KT-555-457

SIMON &
SCHUSTER

ALSO BY DR. BOB ROTELLA

Your 15th Club
The Golfer's Mind
Putting Out of Your Mind
Life Is Not a Game of Perfect
The Golf of Your Dreams
Golf Is a Game of Confidence
Golf Is Not a Game of Perfect

THE UNSTOPPABLE GOLFER

TRUSTING YOUR MIND & YOUR SHORT GAME TO ACHIEVE GREATNESS

DR. BOB ROTELLA

WITH BOB CULLEN

SIMON & SCHUSTER

London · New York · Sydney · Toronto · New Delhi

A CBS COMPANY

First published in Great Britain by Simon & Schuster UK Ltd, 2012
A CBS COMPANY

1 3 5 7 9 10 8 6 4 2

Simon & Schuster UK Ltd
1st Floor
222 Gray's Inn Road
London
WC1X 8HB

www.simonandschuster.co.uk

Simon & Schuster Australia, Sydney
Simon & Schuster India, New Delhi

A CIP catalogue copy for this book
is available from the British Library.

ISBN: 978-1-84983-733-0

Designed by Carla Jayne Jones

Printed and bound by CPI Group (UK) Ltd, Croydon, CR0 4YY

This book is for my loving mother, Laura Bottomley Rotella. Raising five children, she's been as energetic, encouraging, and accepting as a mother could be.

CONTENTS

FOREWORD

THE UNSTOPPABLE GOLFER

Victories are won in the hearts and minds of men.

—Vince Lombardi

At first glance, "the unstoppable golfer" might seem to be an odd combination of words, like "the inaudible pianist" or "the invisible painting." Golf, unlike football or basketball, has no defense.

But in my decades as a sports psychologist, coaching golfers at all levels, I've come to understand more profoundly the old truism that every golfer has two opponents, the golf course and himself. Winning in golf is winning the battle with yourself by producing the best game that your talent permits on the course you're playing. The only person capable of stopping you from achieving this is you. If you can master yourself during a round of golf, if you get the most out of your ability, then you are indeed unstoppable.

To win this battle with yourself, you must have a good short game. Few of us can blast the ball 300 yards off the tee. But nearly all golfers have the physical ability required to pitch the ball, to chip it, to putt it. If we're not doing those things, it's because we're somehow stopping ourselves. Throughout this book, I'll be focused on the way golfers with great short games think, how they play unstoppable golf. You need a great mind to develop a great short game.

I'm going to be talking about fundamental principles of sports psychology that you must understand in order to have a great short game and win the battle with yourself. If you're winning the battle, you're believing in yourself. You're playing without doubt, without fear, and without concern for what anyone else thinks about your game. You pick targets and react to them without conscious thought. You play patiently. You let things happen rather than trying to force them to happen. You allow yourself to perform the skills you already know you possess; you may even find that you can perform at a higher level than you knew.

While no one can stop you but yourself, it's also true that no one can do it for you. As a sports psychologist, I am very pleased that I can't go help a client once a round of tournament golf begins. If I were to do so, I'd not only be violating the rules. I'd be depriving my clients of one of the essential pleasures of the game. They have to do it on their own. I sometimes kid my clients, telling them that I don't know how the ball knows what a player is thinking, but it does. What I mean is that golf gives a player incorruptibly honest feedback. It tells you how well you have mastered the challenge. It's a great opportunity to learn self-reliance, independence, and self-control. It's a chance to exercise free will and personal responsibility. It's a chance to hold yourself accountable. Every time you play golf, you get to choose whether you'll do those things.

You're going to be reading the stories of many players, some of them players who have won major championships or performed brilliantly at the highest levels of the sport. But you'll also be reading about players at the club level whom you've never heard of. Ultimately, it doesn't matter what level you're playing on. Yes, the money and the attention are greater at the highest levels, but those aren't the things that bring real joy to the professionals I work with. The true joy of the game comes from finding out how good you can be. It comes from enjoying the journey of improvement. You don't have to win major championships to discover this. It can happen in your member-guest or your regular Saturday foursome.

Whatever level a golfer plays at, the ultimate satisfaction is the same. At the end of a round, or the end of a career, the unstoppable golfer can look himself in the mirror and grin, because he played the game as well as he could play it and found out how good he could be.

What could be more fun than that?

ONE

THE SHORT GAME AND WINNING GOLF

By learning how to get the ball up and down,
you will have mastered the art of scoring your best.
—Tom Watson

Unstoppable golf and a great short game are inseparable. If I didn't already know this, I could learn it every April at the Masters.

In the popular mind, Augusta National Golf Club may be a course that Bob Jones and Alister MacKenzie designed to favor the heroic long hitter, a Sam Snead when the Masters began or a Bubba Watson today. And there's certainly nothing wrong with hitting the ball a long way, especially if a golfer hits it where he's aiming. Only a fool would say he'd rather not drive the ball 330 yards into the middle of every fairway.

But I've seen lots of players who can drive the ball 330 yards and yet have never won a Masters, or even come close. Augusta National tests their short games and finds them wanting.

All the grass on and around Augusta's greens is mowed closer than the hair on the head of a boot-camp marine. The greens are so quick that inexperienced players can and do putt right off of them. And the putts on the greens are not nearly as testing as the pitches around them. From grass so short that most golf clubs would be happy to call them putting surfaces, players have to hit pitches and lobs that fly precise distances at precise trajectories and then either check up or roll out, depending on the circumstances. Moreover, the grounds crew at Augusta generally mows so that the golfer has to chip and pitch into the grain of the grass, adding another layer of complexity for the elite player.

These conditions expose a lot of doubt and fear. No one gets invited to the Masters unless he is an accomplished player. But I have had Masters contestants come up to me in the days before the tournament begins and say, "No way am I getting in the hunt this week, Doc. I am not going to pitch the ball from around these greens on national television."

That's an extreme example of the debilitating fear that can infect a golfer's short game. At other times, the effect is more subtle.

A young player I work with was thrilled one year to be invited to his first Masters. For the most part, he played very well, but he missed the cut by a stroke or two. One of his playing partners during the first two rounds sent me a message about my client. The message was: "He's a good kid and a good player. But he needs to be able to hit a high, soft lob off a tight lie."

The truth was, my young client *could* hit a high, soft lob off a tight lie. But when he got to the Masters for the first time, he felt a sudden flash of doubt when the need for that shot arose, as it inevitably did. Mentally, he wasn't quite ready to play the short game that Augusta National demands. He played other kinds of shots in those situations, shots from a ball position closer to his right foot, so he could be confident of striking the ball cleanly. They probably looked quite decent to the average spectator, but these shots too often didn't get him close enough to the hole to save par or make birdie.

Physically, he was ready to play in the Masters. He had the skills. But my client still had work to do to develop the mental side of his short game. He had, quite understandably, felt a little bit in awe of the Masters. That had caused him to start to feel that he had to be able to hit perfect shots to compete there. He forgot that on lots of very good golf courses, he'd won because he'd trusted his skills and let himself find a way to get the ball in the hole.

The player who wins at Augusta loves the way the course challenges his short game. He loves showing off his skills. He loves knowing that his short game will separate him from many of the other contestants.

Trevor Immelman, who won the Masters in 2008, is a perfect example. Trevor learned the short game very naturally, the way I would hope any kid would learn it. He has a brother, Mark, who's nine years older and himself a very good golfer (and now the coach at Columbus State University in Georgia). Mark took up the game at fourteen, when he enrolled at a school called Hottentot Holland High School in the Immelmans' hometown of Somerset West, South Africa. Trevor, who was five, tried desperately to keep up with Mark and his friends. Obviously, he couldn't hit the ball as far as his older brother. Out of necessity, he learned to hit pitches close to the hole and to putt well.

The boys' father, Johan, responded to his sons' passion for golf by building a rudimentary putting green with a sand bunker in the family's front yard. Neither Johan nor Mark had to force Trevor to use the green. Trevor's competitive instincts got him started. He remembers that sometimes he would practice his chips, pitches, and putts for hours at a time. Sometimes he would do it in spurts, practicing for fifteen or twenty minutes, then going back inside the house and watching television. Eventually, he expanded his horizons, hitting pitches to the green from neighbors' lawns. Some of them were a full wedge away and Trevor learned to hit over trees and walls. (Somerset West must have been a kind and tolerant community.)

He did not take a lot of formal lessons. Instead, he learned by watching better players, beginning with Mark. He asked questions. He started watching professionals on South Africa's tour. Ernie Els, for example, showed Trevor how he used the bounce on his wedges.

In 1998, when he was eighteen, Trevor came to America and won the U.S. Public Links championship, which carried with it an invitation to the 1999 Masters. He remembers being dazzled and intimidated that year by the speed of the Augusta greens and their slopes. But right away, he felt confident about his pitching and chipping capabilities. Trevor also could see that the best players at the Masters knew where to put the ball on those complex greens. They gave themselves putts they could hit confidently.

When he returned to the Masters as a professional some years later, Trevor set about mastering the subtleties of those greens. His strong short game gave him an edge at Augusta, and he had a sixth-place finish to his credit when he returned for the Masters of 2008. But he was on almost no one's short list of favorites. He had to deal with an additional irritant that year when his swing coach decided not to go to Augusta. I told Trevor that the same thing had happened to Tom Kite in 1992 at the U.S. Open in Pebble Beach. It hadn't proven to be an insurmountable problem—Tom won.

"Let's decide it's going to help," I said to Trevor. "Your job is to find a way to play great golf even if your coach doesn't come. Just get into trusting your golf swing and playing golf."

Trevor had, by then, developed a very smart game plan for playing Augusta, particularly the two pivotal par fives on the second nine, Nos. 13 and 15. The plan depended on his confidence with his wedges. Basically, he decided that on those two holes, he would try to reach the green in two shots only if he had a 4-iron or less for his second shot. Otherwise, he would lay up and rely on his short game.

The plan was more complicated than that, of course. The spot from which he wanted to hit his wedges to each hole varied with the possible hole locations. For some locations, he might want a high shot with lots of backspin that hit the green and spun back. That would dictate a lay-up to a certain yardage. For others, he might want a lower pitch that bounced once and then checked. That might dictate a different yardage or a different angle.

Not every player would, or could, formulate such a plan. As I've said, there are contestants at the Masters who fear and avoid the shots Trevor was putting into his game plan. But the history of the Masters, while it has its share of long hitters, also shows that the short game can be the key to success. Recent winners like Mike Weir and Zach

Johnson were not overly long. Past champions like the Spaniards Seve Ballesteros and José Maria Olazábal were geniuses with their wedges. Tom Kite had always shown well at Augusta.

Trevor, I thought, had that kind of short game. More important, he had precisely the attitude toward his short game that I love to see in a player. It was an attitude that would help him regardless of the shot he was hitting. **If a golfer has confidence in his short game—if he looks forward to opportunities to show it off on the golf world's greatest stage—it helps him to accept calmly whatever happens on the course.** It relaxes him. No shot, no mistake, is going to upset him. His short game is an emotional shield.

Knowing that, it was easy to help Trevor when I talked to him during that week. **I simply reminded him to do the same things he always tried to do—stay focused on his targets, visualize his shots, commit to his routine, and accept completely whatever happened to the golf ball.** They're simple rules, Trevor says, but they're not easy or simple to follow. **It's been my experience that tournament winners, even in major championships, more often than not are people who simply do those things. They stick to their normal routines and fundamentals while other players let the pressure of the moment persuade them to try something different.**

I recall particularly one shot Trevor hit during that Masters. It came on Saturday at the 13th hole, a hole that Masters winners quite often birdie. Trevor drove the ball superbly all that week, but his tee shot on the 13th left him with more than a 4-iron to the green. So, true to his plan, he laid up to 80 yards. But he still intended to get his birdie.

The hole that day was cut in a small plateau on the back-left portion of the green. It's a very demanding spot because the player has maybe six or seven feet of landing area on the plateau. In front of that there's a steep bank. It's very tough to sink a putt from off the plateau because of that bank. But a player can't miss long if he tries to get the ball onto the plateau. The ensuing chip or bunker shot would have little or no chance to stay on the plateau, leading most likely to a two-putt bogey. Most players who lay up at No. 13 when the pin is back-left settle for a par, because their pitch to the green winds up short of the plateau.

Trevor's plan was to hit a low pitch into the bank in front of that back plateau. It was a shot that had to be precise, and I suspect that a lot of players would have left it short. But Trevor had been planning for the shot, practicing it on the range and rehearsing it whenever he got to No. 13 during a practice round. His mind was clear and his confidence was high.

He relied on his routine. He took his sand wedge from his bag, envisioned the shot he wanted, and struck it crisply. The ball landed in the bank, took one hop up, and settled within tap-in distance of the hole. The crowd erupted in applause. It was as fine a birdie as you will ever see, and it gave Trevor momentum that carried him through to the 54-hole lead.

It's not easy to play from the lead at the Masters. A player who had never won a major would be inhuman if he didn't find that on Saturday night, he began to think of all the ways in which a victory would change his life. When I visited Trevor that evening, he was nervous. I could only try to help him minimize those thoughts and refocus his attention on the same ideas that helped him birdie the 13th hole and get the 54-hole lead: **target, routine, acceptance, com-**

mitment. We discussed trying to give each shot the same equal and relatively low emotional weight, staying calm whether the outcome of a stroke was good or bad. When he left the practice green early Sunday afternoon, I gave him a high five and a grin and told him to go get it—but to stay in the present moment.

Trevor did. He misfired only once that Sunday, when he pulled a 6-iron into the pond left of the 16th green. His short game and his attitude got him through. He didn't know at the time where he stood in the tournament, since he tries to avoid looking at leaderboards. He didn't know whether the Masters was on the line or not. (As it happened, he had a 5-stroke lead.) He responded just as he might have done if he'd hit the same shot on Thursday morning, rather than Sunday afternoon. He reminded himself to stay calm. That 6-iron shot was gone, and he had to accept it just as completely as he'd accepted the brilliant pitch to the 13th green on Saturday. He dropped a ball on the front of the tee box and relied again on his short game. He hit a 9-iron over the pond, two-putted, and moved on.

It wasn't until he had marked his ball on the 18th green that Trevor decided to find out where he stood. He asked his caddie, Neil Wallace.

"You're three ahead of Woods," Neil informed him.

Instantly, Trevor went from having complete peace of mind to wondering how he could avoid five-putting. It was a good lesson for him in staying in the moment. He gathered himself, though, two-putted, and claimed his green jacket.

I've coached the winners of 74 major championships on the PGA, LPGA, and Champions tours. Trevor was the first, and to date the only, one who hit the ball extremely well all week long. He was near the top of the driving statistics and the greens-in-regulation figures that week. Even given that, I would say that Trevor's short game and his mastery of those daunting Augusta greens were largely responsible for his victory. The critical role of the short game has been even more apparent with most of the major winners I've worked with. They have all hit the ball badly at least occasionally during their triumphant weeks. They have won because of their short games, their mental toughness, and the fact that few contenders in big events play their normal games.

In fact, most weeks on the PGA Tour, the winner does not win as he might have once dreamed he would. He doesn't hit every fairway, knock every iron shot close, and sink a lot of tap-in birdie putts. Instead, he scrambles and putts well.

As I write this, the Tour leader in greens hit in regulation is David Toms, averaging a bit less than 13 greens per round. Tied for 100th are Woody Austin and Steven Bowditch, averaging 11.5 greens in regulation per round. These statistics are typical, though the names change. Almost every player on the PGA Tour hits between 11 and 13 greens per round. What separates the consistent winners from those who struggle to keep their Tour cards? The short game.

I see the critical importance of the short game all the more in amateur competition. I work with college players who can hit the ball as well as any professional—on their good days. But all days are not good days, particularly for young players. Some days they can't find the fairway. On those days, college players with great short games find a way to scrape the ball around in 70 or 72 strokes. They stay in the tournament. They help their teams. Players without good short games shoot 79 on days when their long game deserts them.

The importance of the short game does not diminish as the level of play goes down. On the contrary, average players need a good short more than elite players do. According to the United States Golf Association, the median handicap for American men is about 14. This means that the average club player likely shoots a bit under 90. For women, the median is around 27, which suggests that the average female player shoots a little over 100.

When I watch or play with golfers at this level, I see that they generally keep the ball in play and get it somewhere around the green in the prescribed number of strokes. But they don't hit many greens. If a good pro hits 13 greens a round, an average player might hit three or four. The average player's skill with the wedges is tested more often than the pro's.

In fact, the scores of average players generally reflect their short-game skills. If they pitch a few close to the hole, play their bunker shots decently, and convert a few of their many up-and-down opportunities, they can shoot a score below what their handicaps would suggest. On the other hand, if their short games produce a lot of skulled and chunked shots, they're going to post an embarrassing number and wind up paying for too many of their opponents' lunches.

The importance of the short game also grows with a player's age. When I watch my dad and his buddies playing in Rutland, Vermont, I see that none of them any longer have the power to reach most greens in regulation numbers. But they hit it straight. So their scores depend on how well they handle the pitches in the 40- to 60-yard range that they generally leave themselves. For some reason, these seniors all seem to have an acceptable score in mind when they start a round. It might be 85. It might be 100. It's their idea of respectable, enjoyable golf. If they match or go below this number they're happy. If they don't, they mutter about giving up the game. Sadly, some of them eventually do give it up. They could still be enjoying themselves if they had reasonable short games. Age may deprive us of the distance we had in our youth. It doesn't deprive us of the physical ability required to hit a 40-yard pitch.

In general, it's my observation that a golfer's long game—his woods and his long irons—determines the highest number he can shoot. His short game—short irons, chips, pitches, and putts—determines the lowest number. This principle operates at all levels of the game.

If a professional has a good day with his long game and hits 15 greens, the highest score he's likely to shoot is about 75, assuming he bogeys the holes on which he misses the green and has a poor day with his putter. If he has a great day with his short game, he could go very low, way down into the 60s.

At the amateur level, a player of average length who keeps the ball on the golf course and doesn't hit many, if any, fat shots is probably not going to score much above 90, even if he only hits three or four greens. But only with a comparatively excellent short game will that player break 80.

No matter what level a golfer plays at, the majority of his shots will be taken from 100 yards or closer to the hole. And every hole (barring holes-in-one and double eagles, which are so rare that they don't matter) will end with either a putt or a short-game shot: a chip, a pitch, or an explosion from a bunker.

Despite these obvious facts, when I travel to courses on and off the PGA Tour, I see evidence that most golfers don't understand the importance of the short game. Even at facilities with good, modern short-game practice areas, I see far more players on the range working to get an extra 10 yards with their drivers than I see players trying to sharpen their pitch shots.

One reason for this is that the golf industry sells power and the long game. Power and distance move new clubs and golf balls off the shelves. And a lot of people like making full swings and watching the ball soar high and far. I like that, too, and I completely understand it. It's one of the essential pleasures of the game.

But at some point, if you want to improve at golf, you have to accept the fact that it's a game with a score. If you want better scores, you have to improve your short game. The easiest way to take 5 to 15 strokes off the average player's handicap is by taking fewer strokes on and around the greens. Your short game will win you tournaments and Saturday-morning four-balls.

What's truly ironic is that a lot of the golfers I see sweating over drives on the practice range could spend their time so much more productively on the short game. Let's face a fact. If you're a person with average coordination and strength, and your tee shot currently flies 200 yards or so, you're not likely ever to hit the ball as far as the shortest hitter on the PGA Tour. Maybe if you buy a new, fitted driver, you'll add a few yards. And maybe lessons, swing improvements, and practice could add another 10 to 20 yards. But maybe not. And there's a very real possibility that in your quest for extra length, you'll mess up the perfectly serviceable swing you now have. I've seen it happen more than once on the Tour.

But try this experiment. If you're sitting in a room at home with this book, look around and pick out a target maybe 8 to 10 feet away from you. It could be a throw pillow on a sofa or the middle of the seat cushion on another chair. Now close the book and toss it at your target. (If you're reading this on an airplane, I suggest you wait until later and try it in your hotel room.) Don't think about how hard to toss it or the mechanics of tossing. Just look at the target and do it.

If you can hit your target with the book—and most people can—you have all the innate physical ability you need to have a good short game.

What's more, you already have the other basic tool required to have an excellent short game—your mind. Your body may not be able to swing a club fast enough to hit a ball 300 yards. But your mind can be every bit as good as a professional's. Your attitude toward your short game can be every bit as good as a pro's. Your confidence can be every bit as good as a pro's. Your patience can be every bit as good as a pro's.

If that's true, if nearly all golfers have the innate tools to have excellent short games, why do so many players throw away so many shots around the greens? I can think of several reasons.

The first is that players either don't recognize or choose to ignore the importance of the short game. Maybe they've never reviewed a round, analyzed their strokes, and counted the number that they made on and around the greens. More likely, they've done that, but they tell themselves they'll focus on their short game after they've fixed that slice and learned to hit the ball farther.

Another reason is that some professionals don't like teaching the short game. Maybe they don't feel comfortable with their own short games, or maybe they prefer to teach from the practice tee and focus on the mechanics of the full swing. Their pupils get the impression that learning to play better golf is learning to swing better. Swinging better is part of it, but it's by no means the most important factor in lower scores.

Finally, some golfers have developed such a phobia about their short games that they prefer not to think about them or practice them at all. They've effectively given up and surrendered to what they call the yips.

When I first started counseling golfers some three decades ago, I worked with a lot of players who told me they had the yips with the putter. Nowadays, because of long putters, belly putters, claw grips, and the like, golfers who start to miss a lot of short putts have work-arounds they can use to address their problem. Bernhard Langer is an example of a professional who has been successful for almost 40 years by resorting to different putters and grips. Nowadays, I have a lot more clients come to me with cases of what they call the chip yips. Later on in this book, I'll teach you how to cure this problem.

For reasons I will also go into later, I don't care for the term "yips." Right now, suffice it to say that there are a lot of golfers out there who play in fear of one or another aspect of the short game. For high handicappers, it's likely to be sand shots. Better players tend to find sand shots relatively easy but have mental problems with delicate pitches from tight lies.

Why have the demons of golfing doubt and fear lodged themselves in the wedges? There are a couple of reasons. One is that there's no work-around for these shots, the way there is for putting. You can't walk into the pro shop and buy yourself a belly lob wedge that will prevent you from skulling or chunking the ball. You could change the way you grip your wedges, but you'd be unlikely to get much relief from that.

The only work-arounds that have developed for the short game are the ones that relieve anxiety over chips. Fairway grass is maintained very well at most courses these days, so it's quite possible to putt from well off the green, or take a hybrid club or fairway wood and bump a shot with a putting stroke. But when you're faced with a bunker shot or a pitch over a bunker from a tight lie, there's no way to work around it.

These days, players see those unavoidable shots more and more often. That's because of modern trends in golf course architecture.

I sympathize with golf architects. They've got the economy to worry about, for one thing; fewer developers are building courses. And they've got to satisfy clients who tell them they want courses that are "fun and accessible for players of all abilities, but challenging for the pros." That's like telling Detroit you want a car that gets great gas mileage for your commute to work but will also be competitive if you decide to enter the Indianapolis 500.

Architects, trying to respond, have only a few options. They can't generally get enough land to build holes that would play long for someone who hits a tee shot 330 yards. They can't make the fairways too tight, because that would severely affect the average player. So they try to build wide fairways with lots of tees and put most of the difficulty of the course into the green complexes. Greens these days, whether they are on new courses or remodeled courses, have plenty of tiers and swales and humps. They're often steeply elevated, and they're surrounded by deep bunkers and tightly mowed chipping areas. It's hard, or impossible, to run a ball onto them. A slightly mishit shot will leave a player with a very challenging pitch or bunker shot.

Thus, the short game and the golfer's attitude toward the short game become ever more important. Fear and phobia become ever more prevalent. And I get more and more clients complaining about their pitching yips. In golf today, nothing will measure your mental toughness like your ability to handle these shots and short putts. **You're going to need your short game many times during every round of golf. You're going to find out if you trust what you're doing.**

This book will teach you how to master this challenge.

I am not saying it will be easy or that I have a quick fix. It very well may not be easy. Nothing that I teach has anything to do with whether it's easy or hard to do. But if you want to become the best golfer you can be, if you want to have a great short game, one of your motivations could well be that you want to master something most of your friends and peers never become very good at.

My life has been about studying the psychology of greatness, of being extraordinary. I am enthralled with the challenge of showing people how they can separate themselves as performers—not as human beings, but as performers—from all the other people on Earth who play this wonderful game. I love helping ordinary people do extraordinary things. The ordinary comes easily to people. By definition, the extraordinary doesn't come easily. It requires will. It requires discipline. You will have to muster your will and discipline to take advantage of what I know about the psychology of the short game and great performance.

First you're going to have to reflect on how you see yourself.

TWO

YOUR SELF-IMAGE AND YOUR SHORT GAME

I would much rather have my teams overconfident than with a lack of confidence. It is easier to bring a team down to reality than it is to give them confidence.

—John Wooden

Great golf, like great ice cream, comes in a lot of flavors. I work with some clients for whom greatness means winning major championships. But I also work with golfers who have jobs and families and can only spend a few hours a week on the game. For them, greatness may be winning the second flight of their club championship, breaking 90, or just getting around the course in a way that doesn't embarrass them when they play vacation rounds with their spouses.

Every golfer must define greatness in personal terms.

But however you define greatness for yourself, it's vital to develop the belief that you are destined to reach your goals. You must believe in yourself.

I can imagine some readers, at this point, scratching their heads and muttering, "Rotella, you're putting the cart before the horse. Teach me how to pitch the ball better and I'll start winning some tournaments, and then I'll believe in myself."

That's the way most of us are taught to think about self-confidence. We believe that confidence isn't something you develop or control. We believe confidence is something that comes to an individual as a by-product of success. Succeed and you get confident. Win and you'll believe you're a winner.

But if that were the case, how would anyone ever win a tournament for the first time? If that were the case, why would I be working with players who lack confidence even though they've won?

Some years ago, I worked with a player who had a great swing. And he knew he did. "I have a great swing," he would tell me, "but I just don't feel like a winner."

As it happened, this player was already a proven winner. I had seen him win a PGA Tour event by edging a Hall of Fame golfer. He'd been nervous on the last day of that event, and he hit some wild tee shots. But he always managed to get the ball out of trouble and into the hole for par or even birdie. I'd thought it had been a great performance, and I told him so.

"I got nothing out of that," he said.

"What do you mean?" I asked.

"I choked my brains out on every tee shot," he explained. "I have a great swing, and I choked. I guided and steered it all around the golf course. I was just totally lucky. It had nothing to do with me. No matter where I hit it, I'd find it in the woods and I'd have a perfect lie, room to swing, and an opening to the green. I putted badly, but I was always also misreading the break and the ball would go in. I got nothing out of that win."

In this particular case, the player was totally into his golf swing. A lot of golfers are. Unless he hit the ball perfectly, he couldn't believe he had succeeded. And since no one ever hits the ball perfectly all the time, he never felt the confidence that he needed. He continuously reinforced his pessimism.

And he is not the only one. I've heard a player say, "I guess it's just not meant for me to win this kind of event," after he lost a big tournament by making an untimely bogey coming down the stretch. With that kind of thinking, he won't win a big event, but it won't be because he lacks talent or because some cosmic hand of destiny has stacked the cards against him. It will be because he doesn't believe in himself.

Belief in yourself is absolutely essential. Some people look at a successful entertainer like Madonna and think, *I wonder why she even thinks she can be in show business. She's not particularly gorgeous. Her voice is thin and weak. She's not one of the world's best dancers.* All that may be true, but when I think of Madonna, I think of an interview she gave when she said, "I've always been famous. It just took a long time for some people to recognize it."

I don't have any doubt why she's successful.

Now, some people I work with would react to that quote by calling Madonna arrogant, or stuck-up, or full of herself. Our culture, for some reason, is very ambivalent about confidence. We understand that children need it. We praise their finger paintings and give them trophies for soccer participation. But as kids turn into adults, the messages change. By high school, one of the most damaging words you can use against another person is "conceited."

But whether we call it conceit or something else, great performers generally have a lot of it. I read an interview with Beyoncé Knowles in which she described herself as mild-mannered, even shy, most of the time. But when the curtain goes up, she said, she finds her inner diva. George Lopez, the comedian, saw his career really take off when he befriended the boxer Oscar De La Hoya. It wasn't that De La Hoya started writing jokes for him. But some of the arrogance that De La Hoya has in the ring rubbed off on George.

Great golfers, in fact, quite often have a confidence bordering on arrogance about their golf games. I recall Tiger Woods being interviewed just after Seve Ballesteros died. Someone asked him if he and Seve had played together. They had, Tiger said, recalling a few shared practice rounds at Augusta. He remembered that Seve had shown him an impressive array of short-game techniques, hitting pitches and chips with multiple spins and trajectories. But Tiger didn't make his own short game that complicated. He said he just wanted to hit the ball in the hole. And when someone asked Tiger if he had ever thought of trying to copy Seve, Tiger said no.

The answer might have disappointed some of the sportswriters, who would have liked to write about how Tiger had learned from the old master. But it neither disappointed nor surprised me. Great players like Tiger don't think they need to copy anyone else's style. They're proud of their own. The only remarkable thing I found in that statement was that Tiger made it publicly. Most great athletes only occasionally speak frankly about how confident they are. If they did it all the time, it would be honest, but it probably wouldn't be wise. People like their athletic heroes modest.

I face this issue often with the athletes I counsel. When they realize how confident they need to be to reach their goals, some of them recoil. "People wouldn't like me if I were that confident," they say.

I have to teach them two important distinctions.

The first is the distinction between being confident and telling everyone how confident you are. I don't care if a player keeps his confidence under wraps. I don't care if he sits in the media center and tells the press how great all the players in the field are and how anyone can win. I care whether, in the privacy of his own mind, he believes he's the best in the field. He can say what he wants in public.

The second and more important distinction is the one between the way you feel about yourself and the way you treat the people in your life. Just because you believe you're destined to do great things on the golf course doesn't entitle you to be rude or condescending. It doesn't entitle you to mistreat people. A healthy self-confidence should enhance all the relationships in your life, not poison them. Self-confidence is a gift you give yourself. It's not about treating other people badly. Be cocky with the pursuits you care passionately about, be they golf, business, or something else. But remember that you're not bigger than life, better than others, or more important than others, especially your family and friends.

If you're reading this book to improve your short game, you quite likely suffer from a confidence problem. This doesn't mean that you lack confidence in all facets of your life. Confidence can vary from one function of life to another. You may have great confidence in your abilities as a businessperson, a lover, or a singer; that doesn't mean you have confidence in your pitch shots.

Golfers with bad short games generally have bad attitudes to match. They persuade themselves that they have no talent, or they have the yips, and that they're always going to feel clumsy around the greens. They believe they can't learn the short game. This kind of attitude is an evasion of responsibility. It's counterproductive.

You have to get past it. We can't fix your short game until and unless you do. Nothing I can teach you about being into your target, about having a great routine, about staying calm under pressure—all the attributes Trevor Immelman displayed when he won the Masters—is as important as how you see yourself. **You've got to be optimistic. You must see yourself doing it well.**

If that's difficult for you to believe or accept, try to understand first that **you are what you have thought of yourself and you will become what you think of yourself from this moment onward.**

Your brain is a faithful servant. On some level, it remembers all the things you think about yourself. If you think of yourself as a capable player, it is going to try to give you capable shots. If you think of yourself as a player destined for greatness, it is going to try to give you great shots.

I often wish that there were some way to make a printed record of all the thoughts people have about themselves during the course of a day, as if their brains were connected to computers. At the end of the day, a person could take the printout, read it, and get a sense of his or her self-image, because your self-image is nothing more than the sum of all those thoughts. Some thoughts would be highlighted in bold type. These would be the **thoughts that were attached to strong**

emotions, because they carry extra weight in our self-image. The most recent thoughts would be at the top of this printout, because **our more recent thoughts have a greater influence on our self-image than older ones.**

This concept has two important implications when it comes to golf. Since thoughts attached to strong emotions weigh more heavily in our self-images, it's important to let yourself rejoice in good shots and accept unsuccessful shots phlegmatically. Too many players do the opposite. They get angry at unsuccessful shots. They regard great shots with no emotion, as if great shots were as unremarkable as a bus arriving on time. The second implication is that we can improve our self-image. If all thoughts weighed equally, people who have developed a weak self-image would be stuck with it for a long time or even forever. But since recent thoughts are more influential, it's possible to change how you see yourself fairly quickly.

What would your printout say?

Don't make the mistake of underestimating the importance of this question. As I have observed golfers at all levels over more than three decades, I have been struck by how often people shoot the score they think they should shoot.

Great players think they should always be under par. And most of the time, they are. It doesn't seem to matter how well they strike the ball on a given day. If they hit it in the rough, they find a way to get it on the green and make par or birdie. When some of my younger clients play with a great like Tiger Woods or Phil Mickelson, they frequently come back from the round and tell me that they were amazed by what happened. They hit the ball just as long as Tiger or Phil. They hit it straighter. But they didn't score as well. (This reflects the importance of the short game as well as the importance of self-image. Phil and Tiger both have great short games.)

Other players tend to think of themselves as people who shoot around par, or shoot in the 70s or the 80s. If they start playing so badly that they are putting their "self-image score" in jeopardy, they immediately get focused, play better, and return to their comfort level. Conversely, if they start off hot, shoot some birdies or pars, and threaten to go under their self-image score, they generally find a way to lose focus, make a few loose shots, and return to their comfort level.

You know that a golfer's self-image is malleable; it can be improved. It can also change for the worse. Thus, believing in yourself and developing self-confidence are lifelong tasks. I have worked with players who once believed in themselves, faltered, and lost all their self-confidence. Even if their bad patches were due to mechanical glitches in their strokes, fixing the glitches didn't solve their problems. They also had to repair their self-image by changing the way they thought about themselves.

Quite often, players have to rebuild their self-image when they step up to a higher level of competition. There is nothing that will test a young player's self-confidence quite like walking onto the practice tee at a PGA Tour event for the first time. Suddenly, it seems that everyone hits the ball beautifully. Over in the short-game area, everyone hits great pitches and bunker shots. On the practice green, it seems like everyone is rolling 15-footer after 15-footer into the hole. Suddenly, he hasn't got the best-looking game in town.

I remember working with a young pro whose wife took an interest in our sessions and told me, "It seems so strange that my husband has to work on his confidence with you. When I met him, back in college, he was completely confident."

This wife was a good-looking woman, confident about her appearance. I wondered, though, what might happen if she left her normal social circle and went to work as, say, a receptionist at the Ford Modeling Agency. She would be surrounded all the time by women considered to be the most beautiful in the world. They would be the ones photographers wanted. She would be the one answering the phones. How long would she feel confident about her looks in those circumstances?

Nearly all professional athletes face an analogous challenge.

I work with basketball players who were always the go-to guys in high school and college. When the game was on the line, the coach called a play that put the ball in their hands. These players wanted that critical shot. They wanted to be on the foul line with seconds left on the clock and the game hanging in the balance. More often than not, they came through. If they hadn't, they wouldn't have been drafted by the NBA.

But when they got to pro basketball, things changed. Maybe someone else was already the go-to guy. Maybe the coach of the pro team didn't believe in them and encourage them as the high school and college coaches did. In college, if the player had missed a few shots, the coach just said, "Keep shooting. They'll start falling. I believe in you." In pro ball, if the player missed a few shots, the coach yanked him and set him down on the end of the bench. In practice, the coach told him he had to "accept his role," passing the ball to the team's stars.

Pretty soon, the player who was so confident in college started to see himself as limited and deficient. And this was immediately reflected in his physical performance. There is no difference between a free throw in the NBA and a free throw in high school. But the player who confidently drained the clutch free throws in high school and college starts missing them if he happens to be fouled during the waning moments of an NBA game—unless he's maintained his belief in himself.

That's how self-image can affect performance. Yes, players in the NBA are bigger and faster than most of the players on the college level. And that will have an effect on some players' ability to score, rebound, and defend. But it doesn't affect free throws. Confidence affects free throws.

Playing golf is similar to shooting free throws, in that there is no defender and the player initiates the action. And I see golfers having analogous problems when they step up to a new level. Maybe it's going from the juniors to college, or from college to the professional ranks. With each step, a player has to find ways to retain the confidence that helped him succeed at the previous level. If he can't, he'll likely flounder. It won't necessarily be because the competition is so much better. The player who can't keep growing in confidence will find that his playing skills deteriorate. Putts he once made unconsciously will become excruciating ordeals—and be missed.

Something similar happens with golfers on the amateur level. There's always another, seemingly higher level of competition. You may go from playing informally with friends to playing in club tournaments. You may move from club events to tournaments on the city, county, state, and national levels. You will need to bring your confidence with you at all levels. **You have to be able to believe in**

yourself when no one else believes in you or sees exceptional talent in you.

I participated in a clinic recently that involved playing a nine-hole scramble with the attendees. One member of my group was a man I will simply call Alan (not his real name). After a very distinguished career, he was determined to improve his golf game, even though he was well past seventy.

Five or six holes into this scramble, Alan hit his favorite club, a hybrid 3-iron, onto the green from about 160 yards.

"Great shot, Alan," I said. He beamed.

On the next hole, we used his putt. I complimented him again. I could see a sense of confidence developing in him in much the same way I can see a balloon filling with air. His posture changed. His demeanor changed.

On the 8th hole, a par three, Alan again hit his hybrid onto the green, maybe five feet from the hole. I slapped his back. We used his shot. "Your birdie, Alan," I said, giving him the first putt. Sure enough, he drained it. He couldn't have been more pleased. Neither could I. But what I had been doing for Alan, encouraging him—building up his confidence—was something he needed to learn to do for himself. And it was something he was quite capable of doing, if he understood how.

We are all selective in what we remember and pay attention to. Alan usually paid little or no attention to his good shots, mentally shrugging them off as just something he was supposed to do. But Alan paid attention when I complimented him, probably because I was a new voice and I had been introduced to him as an expert instructor. His self-image, accordingly, improved. His confidence rose.

This confidence didn't transform him physically. He didn't start hitting 300-yard drives instead of his usual 200 yards. He just found his A game.

I think of Alan when I talk to clients or clinic guests about self-image and someone responds, "Yeah, Doc, but I just think about the things that happen to me during the day. I don't control a lot of that, so I can't control my self-image."

Many people go through life that way, believing that their poor self-image is not their fault. They think they just let life do what it will and life creates their self-image.

But think about it. We have free will. Like Alan, we can choose what we pay attention to. We can choose what we think of ourselves. Free will enables us to control our own self-image.

Here are seven things your free will enables you to do to improve your self-image:

PULL THE GOOD FROM EACH EXPERIENCE

Suppose you just played a round of golf in which you and your partner were one down going to the 17th hole. Your partner, who has a lower handicap, was steady for 16 holes, and so were you. In fact, you were better than that. You won several holes for your side with good chips and pitches. But on No. 17, your partner hooked one out of bounds off the tee. That left the hole in your hands, and you managed to get near the green in the regulation two shots. But then you skulled your pitch to the green and your team lost the match, 2 and 1. Your partner grimaced, and you felt terrible. It's a painful memory, to be sure, made more damaging by the fact that memories to which we attach strong emotions tend to stay in our minds longer.

But the reality remains that you also made a lot of good, or at least acceptable, short-game shots during the course of that match. Now that the round is over, what are you going to choose to remember and dwell on? Many golfers will take away only the painful memory of that bad pitch on the 17th hole. They don't believe they have any choice about what they dwell on.

But the successful golfer will refuse to dwell on the one bad shot. He will give it a few moments of attention so that he can learn from it:

Yeah, I was worrying about hitting a bad pitch there on 17. I got really tight and really scared and started worrying about what my partner would think of me if I didn't come through. Nobody could hit a good pitch in that frame of mind. But I hit a lot of good shots today when I had my mind where it needs to be. So I have the ability. Now the question is whether I am going to develop the discipline and trust to let myself do it more of the time. I know I can.

This type of thinking is the fundamental component of a trait called psychological hardiness. It applies not just to golf but to all sorts of life situations. A psychologically hardy adolescent, for example, might fall in love and then have his heart broken when the relationship ends. He'll think, *Hey, I was attractive enough to get a wonderful girl interested in me.* He'll analyze any mistakes he might have made with his girlfriend, and then he'll move on, confident that another relationship will come along, and that when it does, he'll be a better boyfriend. The adolescent who isn't hardy, on the other hand, will think, *There must be something terribly wrong with me,* and be afraid to get close to another girl, fearful that his heart will only be broken again.

The successful golfer is psychologically hardy. She will make certain to think and think again about the good shots she hit. She'll analyze her mistakes, learn from them, and then stop thinking about them. She'll remind herself again and again that she is capable and she will improve. And at the end of the day, she'll have the sort of self-image that will enable her to improve.

That's part of what I mean by using free will to control your self-image. Psychological hardiness is, more than anything, a choice. You decide how you're going to think, how you're going to perceive what happens in your life. You may think this is difficult, but it is one of the things that great golfers do. They remember their good shots and their triumphs.

PUT ASIDE THE MEMORY OF MISTAKES

When you make a mistake, learn from it, then put it aside. Great athletes do this, and they do it despite a media environment that makes forgetting mistakes much tougher than it is for the average golfer. If you make a mistake on the last hole of your Saturday match, no one will be talking about it by Saturday evening unless you do. If you falter on one of golf's great stages, reporters will be bringing it up for the rest of your life. Yet great athletes put such memories aside.

This trait can be learned. Michael Jordan has written about how he used to think he was supposed to brood for long periods of time when he did something wrong on the basketball court. Then his college coach, the great Dean Smith, set him straight. He told Jordan to think about errors only long enough to learn from them, then forget them. If he wanted to think about basketball any more, Smith told Jordan, he should think about playing great in the next game.

Not everyone understands this principle as well as Dean Smith did. Some coaches think they have to berate their players repeatedly in order to coerce them into playing better. A lot of athletes think that if they don't brood about their mistakes, and brood at length, people will think they don't care, that they're not trying to win. I heard that recently when the Dallas Mavericks beat the Miami Heat in the NBA finals. Some commentators expressed outrage when they learned that several of the Heat players went out and partied after the final game.

These commentators no doubt never give a second thought to why their predictions on the outcome of the Super Bowl, the World Series, or the U.S. Open are so consistently wrong. But they are dead certain that they know basketball players who have lost in the finals ought to spend the next few months seething in a deep funk.

In fact, the opposite is true. An athlete who quickly moves on after making a mistake, who forgets it and retains his optimism, is doing what it takes to win. Someone who sits and rehashes a mistake over and over again is ingraining that mistake into his self-image. So, once the Heat players had learned what they could from their loss, why shouldn't they have gone out and let off some steam?

You may think that you don't control your memories, that once something happens to you, the memory is locked in your brain, beyond your control. This may or may not be true; we don't yet know enough about the neuroscience behind memory to be sure.

But it is clear that you control which memories you choose to relive. A memory may pop into your mind, just as a salesman may call you at home during dinner. But you don't have to entertain the memory any more than you have to listen to an unwanted sales pitch just because you picked up the phone. You can hang up on the salesman. You can dismiss the memory by choosing to think of something else.

Good athletes have developed different ways of imagining their memories to help them control their thoughts. Some imagine an MP3 player. When it starts playing a tune they don't like, they switch to another tune. Others imagine a file drawer. When an unwanted memory imposes itself, they put it in the drawer and close it.

BE A CHEERLEADER FOR YOURSELF, NOT A CRITIC

I am a big fan of cheerleaders. They are always positive, always trying to boost their team's athletes. I've never run into a cheerleader who criticized a performance. You can have the worst game of your life and as you run off the field, the cheerleader will tell you how great you played.

We all need cheerleaders. You are your team's athlete. You need to perform the cheerleader function for yourself. You need to surround yourself with people who, if they talk about your golf game at all, will be cheerleaders, too.

Too often, golfers do the opposite. They work hard on their games, but then they brood about their perceived shortcomings. They come home from the golf course and berate themselves for their poor pitching skills, or they pick apart their putting strokes. They are setting themselves up to fail, because they think about failure.

Quite often, these golfers are able to understand that berating and nagging don't work in other contexts. They would be quick to object if a third-grade teacher mercilessly criticized one of their children. They would get a divorce rather than live with a spouse who constantly picked out flaws and nagged. But they do the same thing to themselves when it comes to golf.

Again, there is a strain in our culture that tells us that it's helpful to berate yourself, to focus on your shortcomings. This is perceived to be honest and mentally tough. It's supposed to be part of the will to win.

But I think back to something I heard Bob Knight say in a television interview a while ago. Knight said that after years of coaching, he'd finally learned something his wife had been trying to tell him for a long time—he could criticize too much. "My wife has convinced me that I have hurt, ruined, even lost players because of this," I remember Knight saying. "She tells me that the players don't make mistakes on purpose or to irritate me. When a player makes a mistake, he knows it, and if I am going to get on him, I ought to just make sure he understands how he can improve, then let him play basketball."

I suspect that the media image of Bob Knight is misleading, because it consists almost entirely of Bob Knight the berater. I think he must have had another side as a coach, a side that instilled confidence, at least in some of his better players.

I know that great players have ways of cheering themselves on. Greg Norman once told me that when he was a boy in Australia, learning to play golf well, there was a popular song with lyrics that went, "Keep on singing, don't stop singing, you're going to be a star someday." Greg changed the words slightly, to "Keep on swinging, don't stop swinging, you're going to be a star someday," and he would sing this to himself as he practiced.

Music, in fact, can be a helpful part of cheering for yourself and developing your self-confidence. Years ago, when I was the director of sports psychology at the University of Virginia, I counseled twins, Lisa and Leslie Welch, who were members of Virginia's national-champion women's cross-country team. They used a song called "Another One Bites the Dust" to rally themselves as they ran, humming it each time they passed a rival runner.

TRAIN YOUR MIND AT NIGHT

You can practice your physical skills only for a limited amount of time each day. For a twelve-year-old in the summertime, the limit may be quite loose. Kids can and do spend hour after hour hitting golf balls, which is great. But the time available for physical practice tends to change in inverse proportion to our age. People in their twenties and thirties have conflicting obligations, like careers and families. People in their retirement years can find that their bodies break down if they try to spend hours on the practice range.

But there's another block of time available to improve your golf by improving your self-image and confidence, if you have the discipline and determination to make use of it. At night, you can become the Steven Spielberg of your life story. You get to write it and choose whether you're the star in a story with a happy ending.

Some of my clients react skeptically to this advice. They're willing to spend hours at physical practice, but the idea of spending time at night working on their minds is alien to them. They don't think "normal" people engage in such activities. Or they think that it amounts to daydreaming, which they associate with lazy people and losers. All I can say is that "normal" people don't win golf tournaments, either. Working this way can be very helpful. It may not be easy for a lot of people. But very few worthwhile things come easily.

I like to see golfers spend some time remembering and reliving the good shots they've recently made. Some of my clients have found it helpful to write a diary that recounts all of their best shots, even if they come in practice. Some like to use a video of their best swings and replay it on a computer over and over again. Some simply think about their achievements. Whichever method you choose, you'll be feeding your subconscious lots of positive images that it can call on when faced with future challenges.

If you chose one of these methods, take it seriously. A lax, half-hearted effort at mental practice is not much different from day-dreaming. It does no more good than a lax, halfhearted attempt to practice a few chip shots. Be consistent. Be persistent.

VISUALIZE SUCCESS

Some of the players I work with are winners of major championships. But a lot more of them are striving to reach that level. I would never tell them that it's easy. I would never tell them that it's not easier to win once you've won. It is, or at least it can be. Coming down the stretch of a golf tournament, it's an advantage to be able to draw on memories of success in a similar situation, particularly recent memories. (As I've discussed, not all players who have won take advantage of this possibility.)

But week after week on the PGA Tour, the LPGA Tour, and around the world, players win for the first time. Even on the Champions Tour, there are players who never won on the PGA Tour who win for the first time, beating players who bested them for thirty years. Their successes prove that you don't have to experience winning in order to win. One way players make this leap is psychological preparation through visualization.

When a player tells me that he finally got into the final group of the final round on, say, the Hooters Tour but felt uncomfortable and didn't play well, I often advise him to try this technique.

I want you to visualize winning at night as if it is happening to you in the present moment. Try to imagine the input from all your senses—the colors of the grass, the noise of the crowd, the smell of the wind, the sweat on your palms. See yourself coming down the last three holes, staying calm, sticking with your routine, hitting the shots you need. Imagine hitting great recovery shots, salvaging pars and birdies with smart golf and a solid short game. I don't want players thinking of outcomes when they're actually on the golf course. But at night, I want them to think of outcomes—successful outcomes. Imagine yourself shaking the hand of your playing partner after winning, getting the trophy, even making an acceptance speech. Imagine the whole process with as much detail as you can muster.

A surprising number of players have trouble doing this. And there tends to be a high correlation between not being able to imagine winning and not winning. Do it over and over again till you're comfortable with the process of winning. If you can't do it in your mind, how are you going to be able to do it in life?

Visualization is, in effect, a way to train your brain. Your mind doesn't always differentiate between real and imagined experience. That's why, the first time you saw a horror movie, your hair stood on end and you felt other physical symptoms of fear. Your brain responded to the movie just as it would have responded to an actual attack by a vampire. Over time, you learned the difference between movies and real life, and when you went to horror movies, your conscious brain put up a defensive scrim through which you watched. This scrim said, "What we're going to be seeing is not real. There's nothing to worry about."

When you visualize success, you don't want this sort of scrim, because you want the brain to perceive the input as real. So take the process seriously. Most successful visualizers tell me they find a dark, quiet room. They lie down or recline in a chair. They eliminate any possible distractions, from cell phones to televisions. They apply themselves to visualization just as they apply themselves to swing practice.

TAKE MORE PRIDE IN THE PROCESS THAN THE OUTCOME

No one absolutely controls the outcome of a golf competition. You can play brilliantly, but someone else can play even better. You can come to the 12th hole at the Masters with a one-shot lead on Sunday, strike a perfect 9-iron, and have a gust of wind blow your ball back into Rae's Creek. You can play your best round of the year in the second flight of the club championship and lose to someone with more handicap strokes. If you play well consistently, of course, you'll eventually win your share. But in any given competition, there are no guarantees.

That's why I advise players to attach their self-image and their self-confidence to process rather than outcomes. What does this mean?

Your process is all the things that you commit to doing to enable you to play your very best golf. It involves your physical and mental preparation—how much and how well you practice both your physical and your mental skills. It involves the way you play. I'll be talking in greater detail later on about your pre-shot routine, but for now, I will tell you that **the more important question is not how many strokes you took but whether you went through your mental and physical routine on every shot, whether you had your mind where you wanted it to be before every swing.** If you can honestly say that you fulfilled the commitments you'd made to yourself about preparation and you stuck with your routines during competition, then you have reason to be proud and confident.

Other sports share this attribute. I watched David Feherty interview Dallas Cowboys quarterback Tony Romo recently on the Golf Channel. David asked Tony about the common threads that bind football and golf. In football, Tony said, if you've just thrown two interceptions and your team has lost the lead, it's analogous to making a couple of front-nine bogeys to lose the lead on Sunday afternoon. Your response must be the same. "You have to disregard everything that's happened and go with the process that gives you the best chance to win," Tony said.

Even more than in football, a golfer can control the process. (There are no linebackers blitzing from the blind side in golf.) Doing so leads to a stable, quiet confidence.

CONTROL CONVERSATION

The practice greens and ranges of PGA Tour events are hothouses for golf talk and gossip, and not all of it is beneficial. People are constantly asking players things like "How's your putting?" This happens especially if people know that the player missed a few short ones the day before. Most of them mean well. But spoken thoughts, like any thoughts, contribute to an individual's self-confidence and self-image.

I counsel players to control these conversations. The best way to control most of them is to shut them down with a cheery, positive response: "Great!" or "Coming along real well."

Most people will change the subject if you tell them you're putting great. That's because they're most likely interested in one of two things. Either they want to offer you a tip, or they want to commiserate. Neither one will likely help you.

If you respond to the question by saying, "Not so good. Missed a few short ones today," you're likely to hear someone say, "You should try . . . ," and then offer all manner of advice. I am continually amused by how many absolute duffers will, if given the opportunity, offer a professional advice on how to putt, chip, or pitch the ball.

I am shocked and appalled, however, at how many professionals will listen to such advice.

And if you don't hear some unsolicited advice when you allow that your putting is unsatisfactory, you're likely to hear, "You think yours is bad, you wouldn't believe how many times I three-jacked it yesterday." Some individuals seem intent on proving that misery loves company, and they'll gladly swap stories of missed putts for hours if you let them.

There's a reason why the late Harvey Penick advised young tour pros to go to dinner only with good putters. Conversation matters. If you're going to talk about golf, talk in ways that will build your confidence, not undermine it. Talking about bad putts or bad pitches reinforces memories you'd be better off ignoring.

Obviously, you have to talk candidly with your teacher. But even then, try to begin your conversations by making note of things you've done well and ways in which you're improving. And choose a teacher who is similarly positive and constructive.

Sometimes a player will tell me, "Yeah, it's easy for someone like Tiger Woods or Rory McIlroy to be self-confident, but I didn't win everything when I was a kid like they did. I am going to have to build confidence gradually."

There's no question that the ideal route to a confident, helpful self-image would involve lots of early success. But not everyone can have that type of early, sustained success. And while a player can control his thoughts and develop self-confidence, there's also no question that at some point, it helps a lot to see some results. Winning is, or should be, a strong reinforcement.

So I understand that for nearly all golfers, the process of building confidence and a strong golfing self-image will be a slow and steady one. It's not going to be a road-to-Damascus experience wherein a player sees a sudden, blinding light and turns from self-doubt to self-confidence.

It will be, rather, a process of continuous improvement. Players who reach their goals generally work simultaneously on all facets of their games, mental and physical. They may not start off believing they can win major championships, or club championships, but they get there. They understand that developing confidence is not a passive process, any more than developing a good short game is a passive process. They don't wait for results to give them confidence. They work at it.

They understand that golfers can delude themselves if they practice only their physical skills, play in a tournament without being confident and trusting themselves, then use the results of that tournament to evaluate themselves. That creates a negative cycle. Golfers generally don't play well if they don't believe in themselves and trust their skills. Why would they blame their swings if they swung with doubt? If they base their self-image on such tainted results, they'll never improve. The only way to assess your mechanics accurately is to get your head in the right place, then see how you do.

THREE

LOVING YOUR SHORT GAME

You've got to defend, dive on the floor, take charges, and rebound. Those are the staples of how we play.

—John Calipari

Back in 1905, the great English golfer Harry Vardon wrote one of the game's first instruction books, *The Complete Golfer*. He began the chapter on driving with the observation that British golfers of the day suffered from "a debauchery of long driving." Vardon wrote, "There is a tendency to regard a very long drive as almost everything in the playing of a hole and to be utterly careless of straightness and the short game."

A century later, Harry Vardon would probably notice only one big change in golf. The distances players strive for have grown dramatically. Vardon wrote about players going all out to hit the ball 250 yards off the tee. Now the biggest hitters routinely try to go 100 yards beyond that. But the lust for distance remains the same as it was in Vardon's day.

Let me be clear. There's nothing wrong with distance. Anyone would rather hit the ball 350 yards if he could do it consistently and accurately. **It's the lust for distance that I see messing players up.**

What Vardon wrote suggests to me that had there been sports psychologists a century ago, a portion of their challenge would have been helping players see that they were hurting themselves by wishing they had the game and power of Ted Ray, or whoever the paragon of the long drive was back then. I know because a lot of what I do with golfers of the early twenty-first century is to persuade them to love their own games, even if those games don't feature the power of J. B. Holmes, Álvaro Quirós, or whoever is leading the world in driving distance at the moment. I have to persuade them of two salient facts, facts that were evident as well to Harry Vardon:

1. **Nothing is more important to a golfer's success than his ability with the scoring clubs—the short irons, wedges, and putter. Players with great short games should be the cockiest golfers on the planet.**
2. **You won't fulfill your potential as a golfer unless you embrace your short game, love your short game, take pride in your short game, and stop wishing you had someone else's long swing.**

The truth is that the length you hit a golf ball is probably the aspect of your game over which you have the least control. Distance is a function mainly of equipment and club head speed. Let's assume that you play with reasonably good golf balls and clubs that have been properly fitted for you. The only way you're going to gain distance is to improve your club head speed. It's not impossible to do so. There may be refinements you can make in your long swing. You might be able to go to the gym and get stronger and more flexible. And I would not discourage any golfer from doing those things. On the contrary, I would generally encourage it.

However, none of that will turn Corey Pavin into Bubba Watson.

If you're an average American male golfer, you probably hit the ball between 200 and 230 yards off the tee. If you're an average female, you're somewhat shorter. And it's highly unlikely that lessons, swing changes, and a fitness regimen are going to give you a driving distance equal to Corey Pavin's, much less Bubba Watson's.

And yet, you can hardly avoid the intense marketing of distance. Every new-model driver promises to give you extra yardage. Every new golf ball is touted as going farther. Nearly every infomercial promises to unlock the secret of greater distance. It's no wonder that golfers have a hard time sorting out what would really benefit their games. I'm reminded of the barrage of advertisements for hamburgers and pizza I see on television around dinnertime. It's no wonder that Americans have an obesity problem. And it's no wonder that American golfers are desperate to hit the ball farther—and have a scoring problem.

As I tell the players I work with, even if they could get longer they probably wouldn't lower their scores by much, if anything. Once in a while, to prove this, I will play with someone and let him move his ball up on every driving hole—up a lot. He can pick up his tee shot where it landed and pace off 60 additional yards on the same line. On par threes, he can tee off 40 yards closer. (If you want to try this yourself, and you don't want to be seen at your club picking your ball up and dropping it closer to the hole, just use the course's most forward tees.) Players are routinely blown away by what happens. Nearly all the time, moving their drives an additional 60 yards or playing from forward tees, they shoot just about the same scores they normally would.

For one thing, if you start a tee shot off line and then add 60 yards, a manageable problem—a drive into the rough—can become a calamitous drive out of bounds. But the more important reason that distance doesn't dramatically lower most players' scores is that most golfers throw away the bulk of their shots when they've got their scoring clubs in their hands—their short irons, wedges, and putters. This little experiment reveals the weaknesses in their short games and it reveals how much those weaknesses affect scoring.

Yet, I work with a lot of players, including professionals, who are all but obsessed with adding distance to their tee shots. I can understand this. If you're a player who averages 280 yards off the tee, and you're on the PGA Tour, these days you're going to spend a fair amount of time looking at the back of your playing partner as he waits for you to be the first to hit to the green. There will be par fives that your opponents can reach in two shots while you have to lay up and hit a wedge to the green.

But I have seen player after player get in trouble by lusting after more distance. I see them on the range with what looks like a yard sale for drivers. They've got 30 different combinations of shafts and club heads provided by the equipment company they represent. They've got every ball the company makes. They may be testing equipment by rival companies. They're hitting drive after drive, looking for the chimerical combination of club and ball that will magically give them 30 more yards.

If equipment can't give them the extra distance, they change swing instructors. They're constantly asking other players for tips on how to get longer. They subscribe to the workout-routine-of-the-month club. If Joe Bomber says he's been working on his triceps, they work on their triceps.

Professional golfers, especially short-hitting professional golfers, did not get to the PGA Tour by being casual about their games. They got there by intensely striving to improve. I admire that intensity. But when it's misdirected, it can be damaging.

Players intensely striving for more distance typically start to overswing, which makes them less consistent and less accurate. They generally spend nearly all their practice time on the long clubs and they neglect the scoring clubs—when it was skill with the scoring clubs that got them to the Tour in the first place.

Worse than that, they are falling in love with someone else's game rather than their own. They're lusting after Joe Bomber's swing. And just as lusting after someone else's spouse is not good for your marriage, lusting after someone else's game is not good for your golf.

You know now how important self-image and confidence are to a golfer. How can you feel confident if you like someone else's game more than your own? If you're lusting after someone else's distance, that's exactly what you're doing. You have more faith in someone else than you do in yourself.

Every time you step onto a first tee in competition, you need to feel that all you have to do is play your game. You can't do that if you think you'd rather be playing someone else's game.

And the truth is that if you have a great short game and a great mind, you don't need anyone else's game. You can be what I call a "silent assassin" on the golf course. While Joe Bomber awes the gallery with his prodigious length, you're hitting fairways. While he searches for his ball in the rough, you're hitting greens. On the par fives, you're wedging it close and making birdies. At the end of the day, Joe Bomber still can't figure out how you posted a lower score than he did.

I saw this early in my career, when I worked with LPGA Hall of Famer Pat Bradley. She wasn't a Hall of Famer then. She was a good, but not yet great, player on the LPGA Tour. Though she was not long off the tee, she had a great pitching and chipping game. Her dad, Tom, once told her she could get up and down from a locked car, and Pat wore that compliment like a badge of honor throughout her career. She loved her short game and took great pride in it.

When we started working together, she was smart enough to realize that she needed to improve her putting, not her length off the tee. We worked on some things that I will discuss later on, in the chapter on putting. Once she got the hang of them, Pat became a great putter, and in 1986, she won three of the four LPGA majors. She very nearly won all four.

Pat understood that her short game gave her a tremendous edge. Everyone misses greens during the course of a round. When Pat was in the final group and her opponent missed a green, she could sense the fear and anxiety in her playing partner's demeanor. The other player was thinking, "Oh, my god, can I get this up and down?"

When Pat missed a green, her attitude was entirely different. It didn't matter to her that she'd missed a green. If she'd missed, she wanted to pitch the ball in the hole. If she'd hit a green, she wanted to putt the ball in. It was all the same. In fact, missing a green improved her attitude, if anything. Her thought was, *All right! It's showtime!*

Not only was she utterly confident that she would either chip the ball in the hole for birdie or, at the least, get it up and down to save her par, she also knew that doing so would be like kicking her opponent right in the breadbasket. She knew most golfers, when they see an opponent miss a green, start to hope that the opponent will make bogey and give them a hole or a stroke. When, instead, the opponent makes birdie or par, it can be terribly deflating.

That's why I call Pat's kind of player a "silent assassin."

This isn't a gender-related concept. Mark Wilson, who has won four PGA Tour events as I write this, learned it when he was a boy in Wisconsin, playing in junior golf events. Mark today stands five feet, eight inches tall, weighs 145 pounds, and is about average as far as length off the tee goes for PGA Tour players. As a twelve-year-old, he weighed even less, and he didn't have the length to reach a lot of the par fours he played in junior competitions. But he wanted to win, and he realized that to do so, he had to develop his short game. He found that it could be a devastating weapon in match play. His opponent might reach the green in two, 30 away. Mark would be 30 yards short, but he would pitch the ball to tap-in range. After conceding the putt, his opponent realized that he would have to two-putt just to halve a hole he'd already thought was his. Faced with that pressure, a lot of them three-putted.

The silent assassin strikes again.

Mark embraced the idea of excelling in the short game. Today he finds it can be just as much a dagger in stroke-play competition at the highest level as it was in junior matches in Wisconsin. Among his fondest memories is the 50-foot birdie putt he sank on the 16th hole of the final round of the 2007 Honda Classic, his first Tour win. He tells me that he's decided that at this stage in his career, he's going to "strengthen his strengths." He's not going to worry that he doesn't carry the ball 300 yards off the tee. He understands that he doesn't have to. He works tirelessly on his putting, his pitching, and his bunker play. It pays off.

If it pays off at the highest levels in professional golf, it certainly can pay off in your golf game at your club. If you have a great short game, you'll have 18 chances every round to separate yourself from the competition. You'll have 18 chances to show off. You'll have 18 chances to win holes your opponents thought they were going to win.

More importantly, you'll be doing it your way. I don't know how well Frank Sinatra played golf, if he played at all, but if I had to advise golfers what to put in their iPods, Frank's version of "My Way" would be at the top of the playlist.

Golfers generally don't play their very best golf unless they have a little swagger. As I've said, this shouldn't mean they're abusive to people. It means that they're arrogant, but it's an inner arrogance. When you decide you're going to make short-game excellence the foundation of your golf, you're going against the grain. You're doing it your way. And that's important.

When you're doing it your way, you're more resistant to doubt. At the highest levels, golf seems to me to be an activity invented to see who best resists the corrosive effects of doubt. The vagaries of the game and its inevitable setbacks seem planned to shake a player's belief in himself and what he's doing.

Add to that the fact that the game is flooded with information and expertise. Care to analyze the mechanics of the putting stroke? There are experts who will tell you that the putter blade ought to go absolutely perpendicular to the line of the putt. There are experts who will tell you it should go inside the line, then straighten out, then go inside again. There are those who will say no, it goes inside, then straight.

If you lack a strong sense of who you are as a golfer, this onslaught of information can be very subversive. Have a bad day and there will be no end of temptations to think that someone has a better way to hit the driver, putt, pitch, or strike a 7-iron. Entertaining those ideas is entertaining the seeds of doubt. Doubt is like water trying to penetrate your house's basement. If there's a crack somewhere in your foundation, the water will find it.

This is not to say that you should be satisfied and complacent with your game. You shouldn't. But there are smart ways to go about improving it. We'll discuss the smart ways to improve your short game later on in this book.

I will tell you now that the smart ways don't include walking around in a state of doubt and insecurity about how you play the game. They don't include taking in and paying attention to a raft of ideas and tips from a multitude of sources. They don't include neglecting your short game while you chase after increased length. They don't include changing what you're doing in the middle of a round.

Yet, I see players who will start making changes in their putting mechanics in the middle of a round if they fail to sink anything of consequence during the first six holes. They'll alter their grip, or their stance, or the position of the ball at address. I see players who start trying to guide and steer the ball around the golf course after one poor shot. They panic.

I rarely see such players win. Players who win make commitments to themselves about how they are going to play, and they patiently honor those commitments. They don't always win, of course. But they always have the satisfaction of knowing they met their own expectations. And more often than not, the winner in any golf event is a player who keeps doing what he is committed to doing, trusting that it will pay off.

That's the winning attitude and philosophy, not just in golf but in other sports. You have to believe in your game, love your game, and execute it. Your game must be based on solid fundamentals. I first learned this not from golf, but from basketball.

I grew up in New England rooting for the Boston Celtics. I played and later coached basketball. Watching the Celtics and learning from some very good coaches, I realized that basketball had a winning formula. No team shoots well every night. But some teams won only when they shot well. Some teams won even when they didn't shoot well.

The consistent winners had a few things in common. They rebounded; they played defense; they made their free throws. Shooting is streaky. But defense, rebounding, and free throws never have an off night. They were why the Celtics won more often than anyone else. All the good coaches I have encountered, from Red Auerbach to John Calipari, emphasized these unspectacular skills.

When I started playing golf and counseling golfers, it became apparent to me that golf had analogous skills. Golfers don't always hit the ball as purely as they'd like. They don't always sink long putts.

But chipping, pitching, and bunker play don't take days off, just as rebounding, defense, and free throws don't take nights off. Winning golfers build their games around those skills, just as Pat Bradley did.

If you want to be one of them, build your game around putting, chipping, pitching, and bunker play. Take pride in them. Love your game.

The purpose of this book is to help you understand how your mind and the way you think can improve your short game. In turn, your short game can improve your overall game and your scores. In order to teach you how to do that, I'm first going to give you a brief lesson in neuroscience.

FOUR

HENRY MOLAISON'S CONTRIBUTION TO GOLF

From about 1937 on through the rest of my career, I didn't think about much while making a shot. It became pretty automatic and effortless.

—Byron Nelson

You will not find the name of Henry Molaison in any history of golf, which is not surprising. As far as I know, he never held a club or hit a ball. Nevertheless, I think he deserves at least a footnote in the annals of the game. Inadvertently and tragically, Henry Molaison taught us something fundamental about how human beings play their best golf, particularly the short game.

H.M., as he is known in the literature of neuroscience, was born in Hartford, Connecticut, in 1926, the son of an electrician. As a boy, he liked roller-skating, listening to radio plays, and hunting for squirrels. His friends and family assumed he would take up his father's trade.

But on his sixteenth birthday, H.M. suffered a major epileptic seizure. More seizures followed. It was not clear what caused his epilepsy. There was some history of the disease in his family. In his childhood, he had been struck in the head by a boy speeding downhill on a bicycle. The accident knocked H.M. unconscious and he needed 17 stitches to close the wounds to his face. Some of the doctors in Connecticut thought that H.M.'s epilepsy may have stemmed from that trauma.

Whatever its origin, the disease all but wrecked H.M.'s young life. For a time, he dropped out of high school. When he finally graduated, the faculty would not let him walk across the stage to receive his diploma, for fear that he would disrupt the ceremony with a seizure. He had to abandon his hopes of becoming an electrician.

H.M. sought help from a number of doctors. Finally, in 1953, a surgeon told him that he could end or curtail H.M.'s seizures by removing the section of the brain where the seizures seemed to be located. H.M. acquiesced, and the surgeon removed the part of the brain known as the hippocampus.

There was a tragic and unforeseen consequence to this procedure. When H.M. awoke, he had lost what a neuroscientist would call his declarative memory. He would never again effectively recall facts he learned or things that happened to him; he could only retain information for a very brief time. He had some memories of his childhood and adolescence, and he could still speak and read. But if he read a magazine and put it down, he could pick it up again twenty minutes later and have no memory of seeing it before.

Each night, he seemed to forget completely the experiences of the previous day. He was essentially helpless, and he had to be cared for the rest of his life. Each morning, the nurses and doctors who were his constant caregivers had to reintroduce themselves to him. He could not remember them. He suffered far fewer epileptic seizures than he had prior to his surgery, but he paid a horrible price for this relief.

H.M., however, retained an amiable and cooperative personality. He agreed to work with researchers who were intrigued by the possibility that his memory loss could help them develop new information about the way memory and the brain work. In 1963, a Canadian neuroscientist, Dr. Brenda Milner, published an intriguing finding. While the removal of the hippocampus had destroyed H.M.'s ability to remember consciously, it had not destroyed all of his memory capabilities. (She referred to him by his initials to protect his privacy.)

In a series of tests, H.M. had been asked to perform a sophisticated motor skill test. It involved what is called a "mirror tracing task." He had to draw lines between points in star-shaped patterns, but he had to use a mirror to see his hand, his pencil, and the patterns.

With repeated practice and testing during the course of a day, H.M.'s performance on this task improved. He did it faster, with fewer errors. The improvements carried over from one day to the next. But as each day began, H.M. could not consciously remember ever doing the test before. To his conscious brain, it was a new task each time. Nevertheless, he had a memory somewhere that showed itself in the form of improved performance. He was learning a motor skill, even though he could not consciously remember learning it.

At another juncture, a journalist was talking to H.M. and asked him about the experiments he had been involved in. H.M. said he didn't remember being involved in any experiments. But when a doctor said it was time to go to the testing room, H.M. turned and started in the direction of the room, even though he had no conscious memory of having been in it.

The experiments with H.M. showed that different kinds of memories are "located" in different parts of the brain. Conscious memory, the type that H.M. lacked, required the hippocampus. But memory of learned motor skills obviously resided somewhere else in the brain, somewhere not readily accessible to a person's conscious thought. We might call this subconscious memory.

In performing these experiments, Dr. Milner and her colleagues discovered a scientific basis for something that smart coaches and golf pros had known for a long time—that a winning athlete does not rely on the conscious brain to perform a skill. **The winning athlete relies on subconscious memory.**

The great golfer Bob Jones once famously wrote that competitive golf is played on a five-and-a-half-inch course—the space between a player's ears. But Jones went on to say that he did not mean to imply that golf was an intellectual game. In fact, he explained, possession of an "active mind" is more a handicap than an asset.

Jones understood the difference between attempting to hit a shot by controlling his movements with the conscious brain and swinging with the unconscious brain in charge of motor skills. The latter was, and is, much more effective. Trying to control the swing with the conscious memory centers of the brain, as he put it, "courts absolute ruin."

Other coaches, in a variety of sports, spoke of relying on "muscle memory" when an athlete was engaged in competition. They told players not to think, for example, of the technique for shooting a free throw. Instead, they urged players to let the muscles use the "muscle memory" they had acquired through countless repetitions in practice.

Muscle memory was a slightly erroneous concept. Muscles have no memory. But researchers have discovered that the body of a trained athlete has highly developed "neural networks" that can subconsciously control the body's movements during the execution of a complex athletic skill—like, for instance, pitching a golf ball off closely mowed grass, over a bunker, and onto a green so that it stops by the hole.

The neural networks that govern complex movements of the human body form through repetition. Consider, for example, the act of picking up a glass and sipping some water. You have only to look at the average one-year-old to see that this is not a simple movement. A one-year-old gets water all over his face, his torso, and the floor—that's why sippy cups were invented. But the child practices, and neural networks form to manage the movement. As an adult, you don't have to think consciously about picking up a glass and sipping water. Your subconscious mind handles that task, freeing your conscious mind to manage a conversation with your dinner partners.

Your subconscious brain handles dozens of movements like this every day. When you first learned to drive a car, you had to be very conscious of each movement. You were tense and stiff. The car moved jerkily, particularly if you were learning to handle a manual transmission. Now, as an experienced driver, you pay no conscious attention to things like keeping the car heading straight and on the proper side of the road. You can, and do, listen to the radio or talk to a passenger while you drive. When you reach your destination, you may not even remember having driven there. Your subconscious memory has quite capably handled all of the physical tasks associated with driving the car.

There's a lesson here that applies to golf. My friend Dr. Bob Christina, a kinesiologist and expert in the learning and development of motor skills, says that with any physical skill, the early stage of learning is associated with the conscious brain and what academic experts call cognitive control of movement. We have to think about each movement we make and how to make it. It's a clumsy stage. Then, with more practice, comes an intermediate stage. The learner uses feedback (the way the car moves, or the way a golf ball moves) to refine the skill. He analyzes errors and makes adjustments. He gradually learns to perform the movement with less conscious control. Finally, with continued practice, the learner reaches an advanced, proficient stage where he can perform the movement without conscious control; it becomes autonomous. The subconscious mind responds to a visible or audible cue (such as the sight of a curve in the road) and the body responds appropriately.

The point is that once a skill is learned, it's far more efficient to let the subconscious brain control it than to try to manage it cognitively, with the conscious brain. To turn on the conscious brain during the execution of a learned physical skill is to revert to the awkward clumsiness of a beginner.

Consider, for instance, the act of walking in a reasonably straight line. A child who is just learning to walk can't do this. She's struggling to figure out how to put one foot in front of the other without falling, and she weaves and loses her balance for a while until the needed neural networks develop. But nearly all adults do walk a straight line many times a day, efficiently and without conscious thought. We decide to go to the kitchen, say, and we just go there.

But suppose you're pulled over some evening by a policeman and told to walk a straight line, even though you've had no alcohol to drink. The task suddenly gets much harder, because the stakes are high enough that the conscious brain gets involved. Unlike H.M., you have your hippocampus. You'll start recalling what you've learned about the consequences of being convicted for driving under the influence. Under this stress, you may try to give yourself a little refresher course on how to put one foot in front of the other. You stare at the line on the side of the road and try to force yourself to stay on it. Your muscles tense. Like the toddler learning to walk, you may waver and lose your balance. You may even be relieved when you're asked to take a Breathalyzer test because you know it will prove your sobriety.

The same principles apply to golf, particularly to the short game. Any veteran golfer understands the importance of the short game in his ultimate score. Miss a green, and the ensuing pitch shot can lead to a par if it's good and a double bogey if it's botched. A four-foot putt can make the difference between winning a hole and halving it. Thus, the stakes are clear on nearly every short-game shot, just as the stakes are clear when a policeman pulls you over and asks you to walk a straight line.

And turning on the conscious brain can be just as damaging to your short game as it is to the driver's ability to walk a straight line. **The pitch to the green and the four-foot putt have a much better chance of being successful if the golfer can manage to execute them with his subconscious brain in control.**

I call this "getting out of your own way."

That's what the rest of this book will teach you to do.

FIVE

TRYING SOFT AND SLACKING ON

Trust that your body knows what to do and play the shot.

—Gary Player

In 1984, I was teaching sports psychology at the University of Virginia and working with the Cavalier football and basketball programs. We had some success, going to bowl games and making the Final Four for the first time in the school's history. A basketball fan who was also a surgeon at the university hospital heard about what I was doing to help the basketball team perform in the clutch. He introduced himself and invited me to come over to the hospital and watch him and his colleagues at work.

So I found myself in an operating room as my friend and his team performed open-heart surgery. I stood on a chair and watched as they opened a man's chest cavity during a quadruple bypass. A nurse with gloved hands held the patient's heart up. Someone else was cutting and stitching.

But what amazed me was the atmosphere. Music was playing. Some of the people in the room were singing. The chief surgeon talked to me about his golf game—while he and his colleagues literally held a man's life in their hands.

It took me a moment to realize they were facing some of the same challenges in heart surgery that Virginia athletes faced in competition, and they were dealing with them in similar ways. (Eventually, in fact, the hospital hired one of my graduate students to counsel physicians on dealing with stress, performance anxiety, and other issues I work on with athletes.) While performing the very fine, precise motor skills involved in surgery, the surgeons had to avoid getting too careful and trying too hard.

Their patients and their patients' families would have been horrified to hear this stated openly. If one of your family members is going into the operating room for open-heart surgery, it's natural to want the doctors to be very careful and to try as hard as they can. This is really a problem of semantics, of the limits of the English language. In English, one is either trying hard or slacking off. We don't have verbs to describe the sort of unconscious effort that produces the best surgical results—and the best results on the golf course. "Slacking on" and "trying soft" come close, but on their own they would mean nothing to people.

But the truth is that being very careful and trying as hard as you can are not the best ways to perform surgery. In fact, I learned that even the finest surgeons almost never operate on family members or people they love. Operating on someone they knew and loved, they would very possibly succumb to the urge to be very careful and to try very hard. They know that they do their best work when they aren't emotionally tied to the patient, when they can have the attitude that the guy on the table is just another guy and this is just a routine procedure. They find it more difficult to operate when they are teaching a resident how to perform a procedure, because the act of teaching requires them to be more conscious of procedure, of how they do things.

The surgeons' work practices demonstrate the truth of what coaches have long known about "muscle memory" and what neuroscientists learned from H.M. When it comes to performing complex physical tasks, human beings do best when they learn the task, practice it diligently, then go unconscious and rely on subconscious memory to perform the movements under pressure. If the conscious mind becomes involved in the process, the body performs less gracefully and efficiently.

We have to get out of our own way.

One of my challenges in coaching is to find words that will help athletes understand this necessary state of mind. Some of my clients, including Brad Faxon and Padraig Harrington, have very sharp, analytical, and curious minds. They want to probe, to understand. Talking to Brad one day, I said, "It's hard to use the English language to talk about how quiet I want your mind to be." That may be because until fairly recently, we had no detailed understanding of the layers of consciousness within the human brain. We knew about the conscious state, and nearly all the words in our language that define states of mind were built around consciousness. For states not controlled by the conscious mind, we had the word "unconscious," which most people associated with what happens to a boxer when someone knocks him out. Psychologists in the late nineteenth and early twentieth centuries came up with terms like "subconscious," which are useful but not especially descriptive.

When I talk to golfers, I use words like "oblivious," "nonchalant," "indifferent," "uncaring," and "irrelevant" to try to get them to understand what I am driving at. Sometimes I will describe it as a "white-out." I use phrases like "see it and do it." I talk to players about "going unconscious." These words give a hint of what I am trying to convey, but only a hint. As I've said, I don't believe there is an English word or phrase that does convey it completely and accurately. But golf is a game of unconscious greatness.

There are people, I think, who intuitively understand this idea. Accomplished musicians and dancers, for instance, find this state when they perform. After countless hours of training and rehearsal, a pianist doesn't need to worry about whether his fingers are on the correct keys or how hard to strike those keys or how long to hold a note. His fingers will be on the correct keys and they will strike them correctly. He forgets about his fingers and just lets the music come out.

In much the same way, golfers at their best just react to targets and let the shots happen. I recall talking once to Byron Nelson about his state of mind when he won 11 consecutive tournaments in 1945. There was no such academic discipline as sports psychology when Byron was playing. But after talking to him, I am pretty sure that he had figured out much of what sports psychology is about. He told me that during his streak, he used to come off the course in a kind of daze, unsure what he had shot. I took this to mean that when he was playing at his best, he had the ability to shut off his conscious mind and play unconsciously. Pat Bradley told me much the same thing. When she was at her best, she came off the course without knowing what she'd shot. She was exhausted, but it was fatigue brought on by her effort to stay out of her own way, to keep her mind focused solely on her targets, playing one shot at a time and ignoring everything else.

This is a hard concept for many people to accept and practice, especially well-educated people. For this, I suggest, our educational system is responsible. One of the cornerstones of American education is "Bloom's Taxonomy." It's a ranking of thinking skills, starting with simple comprehension and going on to what educators are trained to think of as "higher-order thinking skills"—analysis, evaluation, and synthesis. Nearly all of our schools and teacher-training programs use Bloom's Taxonomy, or a variation of it. Teachers are tasked with training children to use these "higher-order" skills. Children must display these skills on tests to get into college. Thus, educated people are by definition those most successful at relying on their conscious brains to analyze and evaluate everything. This may be fine for certain activities, like practicing law or solving mathematical equations. But it's not good for golfers. Truly intelligent athletes have figured out when the conscious brain is helpful and when to let the unconscious brain take over.

Golfers, to play their best, have to have the mental discipline to turn off their conscious brains just when the analytical portion of their minds tells them there are a dozen compelling reasons to turn the conscious brain on. Your analytical mind is silently screaming at you: *You're on the last hole of a match you'd dearly love to win and very much hate to lose. You've got a delicate pitch from a lie in the rough to a front-hole location. Everything is riding on it—the match, the long hours of preparation you've put in, the trophy. Don't mess it up!*

All of your life, you've been taught that when the highest priority is "don't mess it up," you'd better think hard and act very deliberately. There's an old proverb, "Measure nine times, cut once." It's been good advice for school tests, architecture, income tax returns, and a host of other challenges. But it's not good advice on the last hole of a golf tournament.

I've worked for many years with David Frost, the talented South African golfer now on the Champions Tour. David came to me a while ago, tied up in knots with his full swing. He told me his problem had to do with alignment. He'd begun to have doubts that when he took his stance, his body was set up correctly in relation to the intended line of his shot. "I don't even know where my target is anymore because I am trying to get aligned right," he said.

We went over to Keswick, a golf course near my home, and I said to David, "You're a great bunker player, right?" He agreed. David had, in fact, won the PGA Tour event in New Orleans some years ago by sinking a bunker shot on the 72nd hole. "I don't even have to practice bunker shots," he said.

"David, how many degrees do you open your clubface in a bunker?" I asked.

"I don't know. I just open it," he replied.

"And after you open up your clubface, how many degrees do you open up your stance to match how much you open your clubface?"

"I have no clue," David said.

"After you take your stance and address the ball, how much do you think about how far to take the club back and how hard to hit it, considering that every bunker shot is different?" I asked.

"I have no idea," he replied.

I could have asked him how much he thought about his swing plane on a bunker shot or the number of inches of sand he thought about taking before his club head passed under the ball. The answers would have been similar.

"So what do you do?" I asked him.

"I just kind of look where I want it to go and hit it, and it goes there," David said.

"Okay," I said. "Let's do the same thing with your long game. Assume that if you put no conscious thought into your alignment or aim and just look where you want the ball to go, you will find your alignment and you won't be distracted."

David did, and within a few minutes, he was striping the ball and very happy with the way his swing and his mind felt.

He just needed to get out of his own way, to go unconscious.

Working with professionals, I find the sand bunker is a useful place to remind them of what going unconscious feels like. In contrast to a lot of amateurs, professionals find bunker shots easy. They don't even have to hit the ball, just the sand. Sometimes I use high, U.S. Open–style rough around the green for the same purpose, because pros play this shot in much the same way they play bunker shots. In both places, the pros' expectations are low. They're in "trouble," after all. So the pros just do it from those lies. They don't think about it. They get out of their own way. (Amateurs, of course, tend to find bunkers difficult and they don't go unconscious from the sand as readily as pros do. I'll discuss this issue later on.)

I see the same unconsciousness in pros when they are faced with a recovery shot that seems impossible, like the one Angel Cabrera made from the pines to the right of the 18th fairway when he won the 2009 Masters. In those circumstances, there often isn't any technique to think about, because the shot is so awkward. There is only the window through which the ball simply must go. Pros seem to regularly pull these shots off because they get focused on their small targets to the exclusion of all else; they go unconscious.

I recall Angel speaking about that shot some months after he won his green jacket. "People ask me how big that opening was," he said, grinning. "I tell them, 'I don't know, but it was bigger than the ball.'" I guess that's one way to reach the unconscious state that leads to great shot-making—get in the woods and give yourself a target just a little bigger than the ball. I don't recommend it as a regular practice, but it worked for Angel.

It worked, I think, because Angel did not simply go unconscious; he reacted unconsciously to his target, that little slot between branches. It's a subtle but significant distinction. I have worked with players who can play without conscious thought, but when they do so, they forget to react to their target. They tend to get loose and sloppy. They're much better if they can keep the target as part of their mental equation. It seems almost contradictory, I know. *How can I not have conscious thoughts but at the same time remember to react to my target?* All I can say is that good players do it when they're at their best. And I have seen many players learn to do it. Like everything else, it takes resolve and practice. **You're looking for a soft focus on the target, not a hard focus. Take a casual look at it. Make the target small, but not so small that you have to squint to see it.**

One way of getting out of your own way is throwing away expectations. The pros, even those who understand the principle of reacting to a target, tend to turn on their conscious brains more on shots where conditions seem to be favorable and expectations are high, such as pitches from tight lies around the greens. When there are no expectations, it's easier to get out of your own way. No one would have been surprised if Angel's shot from the woods on the last hole of his Masters had hit a tree and bounced deeper into the pines. He had few expectations and thus little pressure. His results were remarkable.

But the pitch from close to the green is a shot that seems simple, and one that a pro expects to get up and down nearly all the time. These expectations make it much harder to keep a clear mind. Even professionals can get very conscious, very doubtful with these shots in tournament conditions; often, they're players who pitch the ball just fine from tight lies in the short-game practice area. Under tournament stress, the temptation to use the conscious mind is more powerful.

Pros in other sports get in their own way, too. I recall once years ago having Hall of Fame golfer Tom Kite, Rick Carlisle (now coach of the world-champion Dallas Mavericks, but then a player), and Marc Iavaroni (who played on an NBA championship team and is now an assistant with the Los Angeles Clippers) sitting in my basement comparing notes. Tom said that the hardest shots for him to go unconscious on were four-foot putts and what he called "bread-and-butter" chip shots, the routine kind. He had to fight getting careful on those shots for two reasons. One was that he expected himself to make the putt and chip the ball either in the hole or to tap-in range. The other reason was the feeling that if he failed to meet his expectations he was throwing away a stroke. This is, by the way, one reason why the short game presents the biggest mental problems for many players. You usually have a chance to salvage par if you miss a fairway or miss a green. Miss the four-footer, though, and the consequences seem permanent.

Rick and Marc, who were occasional golfers, said that when they played golf, they felt no particular pressure on the shots that bothered Tom; that was because they had few, if any, expectations of themselves on the golf course. Nor did they have any trouble going unconscious for 20-foot jump shots. But if they had an open six-footer from the baseline, they felt the urge to get careful, to try to guide the ball into the basket instead of seeing the target and unconsciously letting the shot go. They expected, and their teams expected, that they would make the six-footer. In the back of their minds, perhaps, they knew that there was no backboard behind the six-footer from the baseline, and it was possible they'd shoot an air ball. So they tended to get in their own way on those shots.

Amateur golfers may have some of the same problems when they feel they are stepping up to a level of competition that's more significant. I worked with Dave Novak, the CEO of Yum! Brands, on management techniques. He learned that getting out of his own way improved his ability to speak in front of large groups. The idea is much the same in speaking as it is in golf. If you worry about things like where your hands are when you speak or try to make sure your grammar is flawless, you're likely to come across as stilted and boring. If you simply think about your goal—what you want to tell your audience—your speaking improves.

Dave recently called me because he'd been doing a lot of work on his short game in preparation for a tournament at Seminole, the famed club in Palm Beach, Florida. His short game is really quite good, but he was terribly worried that it wouldn't be good in this event. He could see himself going down there and trying too hard. So we had a long talk about getting out of your own way on the golf course.

That's one of the issues that golfers have to deal with. Getting out of your own way would be easy if you didn't care about the outcome of your shot. But you do. You wouldn't be reading this book if you didn't. Since you care, it can be very difficult to get out of your own way. When I talk to players, I sometimes compare it to going naked on the golf course, in front of an audience of strangers. You have to give up things that are dear to you: your conscious brain, your desire to control everything you're doing, your desire to make things happen instead of letting them happen.

In describing this, I sometimes use the word "surrender." **You look at the target, and then your eyes come back to the ball. You surrender to what you see. You surrender to your talent, your skill. You trust that your body will do what is necessary to send the ball to your target. You surrender to your subconscious and you accept that if you do that, you have your best chance to make the ball go where you've looked.**

Mark Wilson calls it "giving up control to gain control," and he tells me that it's the hardest golfing skill for him to master. He's done it. He understands how effective it is. But, like most of us, he likes controlling things. If he goes through a stretch where his putts aren't falling, he has to fight the urge to start thinking mechanically. Sometimes he wins the fight and sometimes he doesn't.

Some players can never quite surrender. Conscious control is too precious to them. They feel almost guilty if they give it up. They can't dare not to care. If you have all your confidence attached to your conscious control of your actions, letting go is not easy; it can be frightening.

Thus far I've spoken of this unconscious state as if it were a black-or-white proposition. You're either in the right frame of mind to hit a pitch shot or you're not. The light is off or it's on. In reality, golfers' minds are more complex. There is a spectrum of states in which a golfer's mind can be.

I see many golfers at the wrong end of the spectrum. When they face a putt or pitch, their minds are cluttered with all kinds of damaging thoughts emanating from their conscious brains. They think about missing the shot. They think about the last lesson they had or the last tip they read in a magazine. They think about keeping their head still and their weight forward and not looking up and their elbow straight. They think about the arc of the putter blade. They think about what their partners will think if they miss the shot. They tell themselves what *not* to do. Don't leave it in the bunker. Don't leave it short. Without realizing it, they maximize their chances of missing the putt or skulling the chip or hitting the bunker shot fat.

This problem has, if anything, grown in the last decade or so. I think the reason is the proliferation of expertise and information about the short game. Years ago, most golf instruction focused on the long swing. If you look, for example, at *Ben Hogan's Five Lessons,* you won't find any advice on pitching or putting. It's all about the grip, the swing plane, and so on. Instructors tended to dismiss the short game by saying that putting was mysterious and that the chip and the pitch were executed with abbreviated versions of the long swing. So when players obsessed over mechanics, they were usually thinking about things like pronation or starting the downswing with a hip movement.

Nowadays, golf has experts in putting, chipping, and pitching as well as the full swing. Often, the advice of one expert conflicts, or seems to conflict, with the advice of others. Not surprisingly, I see a lot more golfers whose minds are at the wrong end of the spectrum when they're around the greens.

The ideal state of mind for a golfer executing a shot on or around the greens (or anywhere else) is the "zone." It's a place a bit like the hints of the afterlife reported by people who have emerged from near-death experiences. There's an out-of-body quality to it. It's brilliant, it's enticing, but it's elusive.

The first athlete I remember speaking of being "in the zone" was the late Arthur Ashe, describing how he beat Jimmy Connors in a huge upset in the finals at Wimbledon in 1975. Nowadays, people in all walks of life, not just sports, talk about the zone. I would not be surprised if the next time I order a hamburger at McDonald's, someone will bring it to the counter and tell me the cook was in the zone when he prepared it. But just because the zone has become widely talked about doesn't make the concept less valid.

In golf, the zone is a place where body and mind are perfectly coordinated and thinking is not required. If anything, golfers in the zone feel that their conscious mind is detached from their body and subconscious mind. They have the sense that they are watching their bodies do amazing things. Keegan Bradley, after he won the 2011

PGA Championship, told me that he'd gone through the final holes and the playoff feeling as if he were watching himself on TV.

In the zone, the body is on autopilot. The eyes seem to be wired directly to the subconscious brain. The eyes take in the fairways, the greens, the targets. The body reacts. But there's no conscious thought about it, no conscious awareness of the process. When a round in the zone is over, golfers often have trouble remembering exactly what happened, just as Byron Nelson and Pat Bradley did.

Golfers have told me they've slipped into the zone for a few holes or a round, then slipped out of it. They haven't known why. I don't either, not with certainty. But in my experience, slipping out of the zone is associated with starting to think about results. A player gets it going, moves into the lead, and starts thinking about the exemption he'll get for winning. Or he starts trying to analyze why he's playing so well so he can repeat it the next day. Thinking of those things, the player leaves the zone. When you get in the zone, you need to ride it and enjoy it, not try to control it.

If I could give you a road map to take you to the zone and keep you there, I would. But I can't. You can't make yourself get into the zone. But you can create the preconditions for going into the zone. You can't force it, but you can make it more likely to happen.

You can do this by getting your mind into the next-best state, what I might call the clear-and-quiet state. In it, you identify a target and envision a shot. Then you clear your mind, switch off the conscious brain, and unconsciously react to your chosen target. There are two differences between this state and the zone. The first is the conscious effort you made to get there—in the zone, there is no conscious effort. The second is that you're more aware of the target than you would be if you were in the zone. But this clear-and-quiet state is still a very good place to be when you're playing golf. It's a state of mind that greatly enhances your chance to let your skills come out. It might even help you find out that your skills are a little better than you'd thought.

Farther along the spectrum is the player who can't quite let go of the desire to let his conscious mind play a role in the process.

"I can't play without a swing thought, Doc," this player will tell me.

A swing thought is a crutch. If you're playing with a swing thought, you're not going unconscious. But many players have lifelong habits that include swing thoughts, and they can't, or don't think they can, break those habits immediately. I offer them a deal.

They can have a swing thought, but only one. It must be connected to their target. And they must use it on every shot. The sort of thought I have in mind is *Release the putter blade toward the target,* or *Take the club straight back along the target line,* or *Turn the buttons of my shirt toward the target.*

The problem with this deal is that not many players can keep it. They're used to playing or practicing with three or four swing thoughts bouncing around in their minds. Typically, they'll start out a round trying to limit themselves to the one agreed-upon, target-oriented swing thought. They do it until they hit their first unsatisfactory shot. Frustrated, they decide to try another swing thought. When that doesn't work out, they try another. Fairly quickly, they're back to the confused, cluttered state of mind they typically have on the practice range, with a welter of conflicting thoughts swirling around in their brains. They've come to the wrong end of the spectrum.

And, lest I mislead you, there will be shots that don't come off the way you'd like. No matter how accomplished you are, no matter where your mind is, golf is still going to be a game of mistakes. Not every putt goes in the hole. Not every pitch finishes at tap-in range. And all imperfect shots are invitations to turn on the conscious brain.

It always surprises me that golfers so favor conscious control as a way to play the game. They may miss shot after shot, but they'll keep trying conscious control. If they're persuaded to try playing without conscious control, it usually takes only one missed shot to induce them to abandon the effort. All I can tell them is that if a player has to hit every shot perfectly to stick with a process, he will never commit to and stick with anything.

Having the mental discipline to keep a clear-and-quiet mental state even when things are not going well is a hallmark of an excellent golfer. He accepts what happens on every shot, forgets about it, and focuses his attention on the next shot. He honors his commitment to a mental process that will maximize his chances to play well. The right state of mind increases your consistency. It makes your good shots better and your bad shots more playable. It's not going to make you perfect, but it will help prevent a bad shot from turning into a bad stretch of holes or a bad round.

As I travel and talk to groups of golfers, I find that many people can accept the idea that playing their best golf requires that they get their minds as close as possible to the zone. They want to know how they can do that.

You already know a couple of the prerequisites. You've got to have a strong self-image. If you believe in yourself, it's much easier to go unconscious. You've got to train yourself to be optimistic.

You've got to love your game, especially your short game. You've got to make a commitment to the process of good shot-making and honor that commitment.

You have to develop the discipline to trust the mechanics you bring to the golf course on any given day. One of the cardinal principles I teach professionals is "train it and trust it." They have spent countless hours developing their skills. Their skills are superb.

Superb skills, ironically, don't necessarily make it easier to trust mechanics. When you spend a lot of your time practicing golf, you can raise your expectations. You can put pressure on yourself. Expectations and pressure can make it more difficult to trust, to go unconscious. But the best professionals rise to this challenge.

They do it, quite often, by **trying to give every shot the same equal and low level of importance, whether it comes in practice or on the last hole of a tournament.** Obviously, a shot on Tuesday in a practice round would seem to an outsider to be less important than a pitch to the hole on Sunday afternoon. But we're not talking about an outsider's reality. We're talking about what a player does inside his own mind. We're talking about the intensity of effort he gives to every shot.

If I were to put intensity of effort on a scale from 0 to 10, with 0 being sleep and 10 being teeth-gritting, red-faced effort, I would say most tournament players are at their best when their intensity level is 3 or 4. That's my observation. But I really don't care what number a player assigns to his most effective level. It might be 2 or it might be 6. The point is that wise players know that in competition, they have to have the mental discipline to maintain their optimal level of intensity.

Good players, in fact, are probably more intense in practice than they are in competition. Tom Kite has one of the strongest wills to win I have ever worked with. On the golf course during competition, he disciplined himself to look and be phlegmatic when a shot didn't work out the way he wanted it to, and to be the same way when his shots were completely grooved. Looking at Tom's demeanor in competition, it would be hard to discern whether he was five under par or five over. But I can remember him in practice one day, under a hot Texas sun. Despite hours of effort, he was not quite able to make his golf ball behave the way he wanted. Finally, he walked back to his golf cart and punched it so hard I thought he'd surely broken his hand. His intensity level had ratcheted itself up well beyond his optimal range, but that was an indulgence he would never allow himself during a tournament.

If any golfer had a right to be too intense, it would be Tom Kite, who devotes himself so wholeheartedly to improvement. I find it less understandable when I speak to a group of business people or club players and hear someone who rarely or never practices ask how he can be expected to go unconscious and play with a low intensity.

"I have three kids and a sixty-hour-a-week job," I'll hear from someone at these meetings. "I can only manage to get out to play once a week. I can't ever get away just to practice. What should I do?"

My advice to someone in these circumstances is to try all the harder to go unconscious when she plays. The occasional golfer who never practices has to begin with the understanding that she needs to simplify her game. She should putt or bump a hybrid club from off the green when she can. She should probably stick with a plain-vanilla pitch shot. She should use it in the bunkers, just trying to make sure she hits the sand before she hits the ball. She should pick reachable targets and not try any Phil Mickelson–style flop shots. Play a simple game.

If you're a golfer who can't practice, you won't help yourself by trying harder, caring too much, or using your conscious brain. If your mechanics are rusty, accept the fact that you're going to be playing with a rusty swing and accept the results. Keep your intensity level low. See the shot, hit the shot. Have fun. Remember that if you can't get yourself in the zone or in a clear-and-quiet state of mind, you'll still help yourself by getting as close to that end of the mental spectrum as you can.

It will also help if you have an effective pre-shot routine, which is something that you don't have to be at the golf course to practice. I'll talk about what that means in the next chapter.

SIX

ROUTINE: YOUR WINGMAN

I drew a few deep breaths and began my pre-shot routine. Suddenly, despite the noise, energy, and excitement, there was solitude. My mind quieted.

—Annika Sorenstam

At the 2011 U.S. Open, a lot of players had difficulty with the short-game practice area. Congressional Country Club had revamped the area in preparation for the tournament, and the turf was new. It appeared that it hadn't had time to develop the normal root structure. Players found that when their club heads touched the ground, the grass seemed to explode. They started hitting the ball fat and skulling it. And I'm not talking about players you've never heard of. I'm talking about players like Graeme McDowell, who was the defending champion. As the competition was about to start, Graeme did not have the pitching game I'd become accustomed to seeing from him. His swings were tentative and careful. He was not making clean contact.

He wanted very much to make a respectable defense of his title. Whether he won or not, he didn't want anyone thinking he was a flash in the pan. He'd been spending a lot of time practicing pitching that week, but the hard work hadn't helped.

"You've been putting really well, haven't you?" I asked him.

"My putting is good," he affirmed.

"Do you have a really good putting routine?" I asked.

"Yeah, I do," Graeme said.

"How good is your pitching routine compared to your putting routine?" I asked.

Graeme almost fell over. "I'd say it's so bad it's like I don't have one."

"Do me a favor," I said. "On the next five or ten pitch shots you hit, I want you to get into your target and use your putting routine." He and I both understood that we weren't talking about the physical elements of his putting routine, but the mental elements.

Graeme tried it. He hit five gorgeous pitch shots in a row.

"That's unbelievable," he said. "I haven't hit a pitch shot like that in a month and a half. When I've tried the last six weeks to work on my pitching, I've always used my full-swing routine. It never crossed my mind to use my putting routine. When I did, it immediately got me out there and into my target. With my putting, I don't ever put pressure on myself by thinking that I have to make it. I'm into my target, but it's like, 'Eh, so what.' But I've been so into my technique with my pitching, so worried about contact, that I've not been even close to being into a target."

I wish that all my efforts to help players could be so easy. Graeme went on to finish that Open two under par, tied for 14th. He didn't win, but he did make that respectable defense he'd wanted. His routine was the key.

There are two lessons to be learned from this. The first is that players have different physical routines for different shots and that a good player's putting, pitching, and long-shot routines may differ from one another. The second and more important lesson is that the essence of a good routine is not physical; it's mental. By using his putting routine when he pitched the ball, Graeme repaired the most basic fundamental of his, or anyone's, mental game: his orientation to the target.

Of course, you have to have a routine. Routine is a golfer's wingman, fending off the dangers of doubt, fear, and distraction. Routine promotes consistency. Routine offers an answer to the question, "I'm so nervous, what am I going to do?" Many a tournament winner has gone to the first tee fighting nerves and triumphed simply by honoring a commitment to follow his routine on every shot.

There are, I know, players who don't have routines. But I never see them succeeding on the professional level or the elite amateur level. A player without a pre-shot routine plays haphazardly. Golf is a game of consistency, and consistency begins with a sound pre-shot routine.

I occasionally run into people who think that the essence of a good pre-shot routine is taking the same number of practice strokes before each shot. Nothing could be further from the truth. I have successful clients who religiously take one or two practice swings. I have clients who take none. I have clients who take one or two or three, waiting until they feel the swing they want. It's immaterial. If the United States Golf Association and the Royal and Ancient Golf Club got together tomorrow and banned practice swings, I don't think it would raise the average score at all. In fact, I think it might help scoring, because there are players who allow doubt or fear to enter their minds while they're taking their practice swings. If they eliminated the practice swings and got on with it, they'd play better.

There are, of course, physical elements in a sound pre-shot routine. Grip, stance, posture, alignment, and ball position are all vital in the success of a shot. Your routine should include a method that will consistently deal with each of these factors, which will vary depending on whether you're about to hit a pitch, a bunker shot, or a putt.

I won't, however, prescribe them for you. There is no one-size-fits-all answer to the question of how you should hold the club and address the ball. I've seen a lot of different methods work. Each player has to work out his or her own style. It's advisable to do this in consultation with a teacher. Finding the answers that work for you generally takes a lot longer if you try to do it alone.

I will say that you should practice your physical routine, whatever it is. Good players have different ways of doing this. Some find a full-length mirror and mark it with pieces of tape that indicate where key parts of the body ought to be when the player stands in front of the mirror and addresses an imaginary ball. Good players, when they're on the practice range, will often use a club shaft or some other straight edge to help them make sure that they're aimed correctly and that, say, the line between their toes is parallel to the intended flight of the ball. **The goal is to learn your address procedure so well that you don't have to give it any thought as you play. Like your swing or your stroke, it should be governed by subconscious memory.**

That said, it's also true that nearly every good golfer I work with regularly supplements his own eyes in checking on the fundamentals of grip, posture, alignment, and ball position. You may be able to eyeball your grip and make sure it's the way it's supposed to be. But you can't assess your posture and alignment as well as a trained professional can. And over time, flaws in these fundamentals tend to creep into anyone's game. They do so gradually, so that a player doesn't notice the changes himself. He doesn't realize that he's slouched over or his shoulders have opened up too much.

Some touring pros schedule regular sessions with their swing teachers to check on these things. Jack Nicklaus used to begin every season by having a session with his boyhood teacher, Jack Grout, to go over his fundamentals. Today, a lot of players and their teachers do these sessions with the help of video cameras. Your method for doing this is not as important as your commitment to doing it and to maintaining good setup fundamentals. Maintenance is something that anyone, even someone with no daylight hours for golf practice, can do. But do it in practice, not in competition.

The mental part of your routine begins well before you address the ball. As you approach any shot, you're sizing up the situation and deciding on the way you want to hit the ball. If it's a full shot to the green with one of your scoring clubs (your 8- and 9-irons and your wedges, for the most part) you're assessing the distance, your lie, the hole location, the wind, and the firmness of the greens. But when an experienced player is at his best, these assessments take place without much thought; though no two lies are identical, for instance, a lot of them are very similar. If you've played a lot of golf, you've seen something very like what you're going to see on any given shot. Trust your instincts to tell you what you need to know and how to react.

It's easier to leave the conscious brain inactive than it is to activate it, then deactivate it. And your ultimate goal is to play the shot unconsciously.

I can't tell you when it's right to make the hole your target and when to aim for a safer objective, like the center of the green. I can tell you that if you're on the PGA Tour and you don't feel comfortable going at most flags with your scoring clubs, you're not likely to be on the Tour for very long. But every shot is different and every player is different. You have to select your target based on an honest assessment of your own game and an honest assessment of the risks entailed with each shot you could potentially play.

I also won't tell you which clubs to use in which situations. I'll go into this in more detail later on. In general, I like people to go with their first instinct regarding club and shot selection, because their first instinct is usually the shot they can see most clearly and easily in their mind's eye. But the most important thing is that you pick a club and a shot trajectory that give you confidence, then commit to them.

Once you've chosen a shot and pulled a club, the heart of your routine begins. At this stage, all good players go into a kind of bubble. Some players like to chat between shots; some like to talk trash. Others are more introverted and find it hard to sustain a conversation during a round. Some people like to think of things unrelated to golf as they make their way between shots. Some people like to notice the flora and the fauna around the course. Whatever your tendency, your pre-shot routine shouldn't allow for any socializing, daydreaming, or bird-watching at this in-the-bubble stage. **For 15 to 40 seconds or so, your focus must be completely on the shot, the target, and your routine.**

You may, at this point, take one or more practice swings. Some teachers call these rehearsal swings, and they have good reason to. You shouldn't, at this juncture, be practicing how to hit the shot. That would be turning on the conscious mind. You're just seeing the shot in your mind and feeling a motion that causes the ball to do what you're seeing. This is why many good players take their practice swing or swings with their eyes on their targets.

Many good players take more practice swings before short-game shots than they do before long shots. If you're hitting a driver, most of the variables are constant—stance, slope of the ground, speed of the swing, etc. No two short-game shots are identical, so the short game is more creative. There are more variables, like the thickness of the rough around the green. There's perhaps more reason to take practice swings, although, as I mentioned, I'm not sure they matter and I wouldn't argue with a player who told me he didn't want to bother with them. It's a matter of individual preference. What's important is that if you do take practice swings, you take them while into your target. You don't use them to instruct yourself about your stroke.

As they go through this phase of their routines, most Tour players I work with are either seeing a trajectory, seeing a trajectory and a spot where the ball is going to land, or seeing a trajectory and the spot where the ball will wind up—in the cup. Some players don't see a trajectory, though; they just see a landing spot or the ultimate target, the cup. On putts, as I'll discuss later, there is a host of other ways that players envision what they want the ball to do. Some very good, veteran players barely see anything—they pick a target and go on autopilot.

But the common element of all effective routines is the impor-

tance of the target. Anything else can vary, but you must get your mind oriented on a target. It should be, however, a soft orientation, like looking at your beloved as you speak over dinner. You're into her, but you're not counting the wrinkles around her eyes or memorizing the shade of lipstick she's wearing. As I've said, make the target small, but not so small you have to squint to see it. Doing otherwise tends to ratchet your intensity level higher than it should be.

Sometimes people will nod their heads when I explain this and then ask, "So I'm fixed on the target and envisioning the ball going where I want it, but then I get upset if it doesn't go in. How do I deal with that?"

It's a very fine line, but while a player should envision the ball going in and be into his target, it's a mistake to expect that the ball will go in. A player at his best sees the shot going in but has no expectation one way or the other about the result. A basketball player taking a jump shot just looks and shoots, but he doesn't tell himself he has to make it or he will make it. When you tell yourself those things, you usually shoot an air ball. It's the same way in golf. Expectations build pressure; they're not helpful.

The next element of a good routine is a certain cadence. You don't want to hurry, but you don't want to waste any time, either. **On most shots and putts, there's a steady rhythm to the last look at the target, the return of the eyes to the ball, and the beginning of the swing or stroke. Look at the target. Look at the ball. Let it go.**

I have a friend, Marty Jacobson, who tells me that this cadence has actually helped his confidence. Marty's routine is enviably brisk. He visualizes the shot he wants, including its trajectory. He sees the ball going to the target. Then he steps up and hits the ball, without practice swings. He feels as if he's creating a direct connection between the shot he envisions and the body movements that create it. As this method has proven itself over the years, he finds himself playing more and more confidently.

I can often tell about a player's mind by looking for this kind of cadence in his routine. If I see it, it's a good indication that his mind is clear and focused. If there's a delay, it's usually because something from the conscious brain has intruded on the process. If you're going through your routine and you suddenly find yourself questioning your alignment, that's an intrusion. If you're going through your routine and you suddenly wonder whether you've got the right club, that's an intrusion. If you stop after your last look at the target and try to remember all the mechanical things you've ever been taught about how to make the swing you want, that's beyond an intrusion. The barbarians have breached the gates, and you're in trouble.

When they get to this stage in their routines a lot of good players tell me they feel almost indifferent, just as Graeme McDowell did when he told me his feeling about a putt that missed was "Eh, so what." They want the ball to go to the target. They're trying to get the ball to go to the target. In fact, they're following a routine they've worked out and practiced to maximize their chances to succeed.

But a critical part of a good routine is acceptance of whatever happens once the ball is struck, whether that be success or failure. I've found that when I try describing this state of mind to players, it strikes some as contradictory. "How can I shrug and accept the ball not going to the target when I've worked so hard to get focused on the target and make it go there?" they ask.

It's a reasonable question. All I can tell you is that the best players get into this state of mind. They do it in different ways. I have known players who remind themselves (not as they're about to swing) that regardless of what happens to a given shot, they will still be standing on the preferable side of the ground. Their loved ones will still love them. Their health will be the same. Their bank accounts may change a little, but in the end, how much does that matter? Other players feel destined to win and make great shots; they just don't know when it will happen. So if a shot misses, it just brings them a little closer to success. Other players reach the attitude of acceptance by a process of reasoning. They understand that they can only control the things that they themselves think and do. Once the ball leaves the club face, it's out of their control. So the only reasonable thing to do is accept whatever happens. Their commitment is to the process, not the results it produces on a given shot. This commitment to the process, not the result, characterizes great routines. Whatever happens to a shot, the player is content if he's stayed with the process.

Regardless of how you get there, acceptance completes your routine. Your attitude has to be, *No matter where it ends up, I am going to accept it, go get it, and score with it.* You must feel that a new game of golf starts at the end of every shot.

Sometimes a client will tell me that he does his best to follow his routine and banish doubts, fears, and distraction on the golf course. But they still plague him.

My response is that nearly all golfers are afflicted with doubt or distraction at some point during a round, and there's no reason to be overly concerned about it. In fact, athletes in all sports have their demons. Jimmie Johnson, the NASCAR racer, once told me that right before a race, he was afraid he would forget how to drive a car. But he always remembered; that's why he's won five straight NASCAR championships. Mike Tyson has talked about how scared he was in the weeks leading up to a fight. He would have occasional nightmares about being killed in the ring. But once he climbed into the ring, at least in his best years, he felt godlike and invincible.

Routine is your defense. The routine of getting taped, warming up, and climbing through the ring ropes helped change Mike Tyson's attitude and made him feel invincible. The routine of climbing into the car, starting the engine, and moving to the starting line calmed Jimmie Johnson down. People would be surprised at how many golfers are like that. They have their doubts and fears at times, but when they go into the bubble of their routines, they are able to focus—most of the time.

No one is perfect at it, except on those rare days when they play an entire round in the zone. But I would say that successful PGA Tour pros get themselves into the right frame of mind 90 to 95 percent of the time. If they can't, they usually back off and restart their routines.

I have seen good players line up for a pitch shot, back off, and reach for their putter or a hybrid club because their routines couldn't dispel the doubts they had about making good contact with the ball. I would much prefer them to do this than to hit a shot when they're fearful of it. This goes particularly for amateurs who don't get to practice or play as much as they might like. Hit the shot you feel comfortable with, even if it's not the shot you see pros hitting on television.

If you're an amateur whose practice time is limited, there may be times when you're going to feel uncomfortable because there isn't an alternative. You have to putt when you're on the green, even if you're in doubt. Even if the shot scares you, you have to pitch the ball over a creek to get to the green—there's no bumping a hybrid. In those cases, the only thing you can do is admit to yourself that your mind is not as clear as you would like. Be honest about it. That alone will calm you down a bit. Then go through your routine as well as you can. A partially successful process is better than no process at all.

Your challenge is no different than the challenge even the best players face under pressure. When a pro comes down to the final holes of a championship he's dreamed of winning but never won, he faces much the same gut check as the weekend player looking at a pitch over a creek to a green for a $2 Nassau.

That's when the pro finds out whether he's prepared to win. Winners are the players who do the same thing at gut-check time that they do during practice on Tuesday morning—their routine. They love being on the stage, love being in the last group, because they have confidence that under any circumstances, they'll do the same thing they always do.

SEVEN

SEE IT AND ROLL IT

Putting is, to a far greater extent than most of us suspect, purely a matter of confidence. When a man feels that he can putt, he putts, and when he has doubts about it, he almost invariably makes a poor show upon the greens.

—Harry Vardon

A year or two ago, I gave Angel Cabrera a putting lesson. He was working on his stroke with my friend Charlie Epps. Angel had won a couple of majors by that time, but he wasn't happy with his putting. He was spending a lot of time on the practice green, but his practice was not paying off in fewer putts or more confidence.

"When I am on the tee box, I just look at it and hit it," he told me. "When I'm on the tee box, I feel like I'm the king of the world. I don't feel that way on the putting green."

A lot of players would say the same thing about their games. They feel secure and confident with full swings. But on the greens they are doubtful, hesitant, and unsuccessful.

This is an especially prevalent problem on the PGA Tour. Not everyone there hits the ball as far as Angel Cabrera, but everyone hits the ball well. Week after week, championships go to the player who separates himself by putting well. The same thing is true in competitions like the Ryder Cup and the Presidents Cup. Both teams are composed of elite ball-strikers. The trophy generally goes to the team that putts better.

I find that amateurs on the club level are a little less stressed about putting, probably because they have other problems with their games that seem to be more serious. When you can't consistently get your tee shots onto the golf course, you tend not to worry about putting. But as amateur players get better, they find that the importance of their putting seems to grow.

No matter what level you play at, you're going to take an average of 27 or more (quite a few more if you're an average player) of your strokes with your putter during every round. That's about twice as many as you'll take with any other club. **Thus, the fastest way to improve your scores is by improving your putting.**

The way to do that, more often than not, is by improving the way you think about putting. In Angel Cabrera's case, I challenged him to think the same way about his putting as he did about his driving—to just look at the ball and hit it. The very idea gave him trouble. People can easily go unconscious when they're very confident about a shot or a club, as Angel was with his driver. It's very hard to go unconscious if you have doubts.

To help him understand this, I took away his putter and gave him a long iron. He putted with that for a while, and putted quite well. Then I gave him his driver. He made putts with that. Then I gave him his sand wedge and he made eight-foot putt after eight-foot putt, blading the ball with the wedge.

Angel grinned. "I think I get it," he said. "You want me to putt with a wedge."

He was kidding. He and I both understood that taking his putter out of his hands had changed his attitude toward the putts he was hitting. With the putter in his hands, his attitude was something like *I should make this, I've been practicing so long my back hurts, my putting is killing me, gotta release the putter head, make it roll right, why won't the ball go in?* With a wedge in his hands, he had no expectations. He hadn't practiced with it. He just looked at the target and hit the ball. He didn't care if he missed. He easily went unconscious because he felt blameless if he missed a putt with a wedge.

That was what I wanted Angel to do when he had a putter in his hands. It isn't easy. When you're putting, assuming you're keeping score, the stakes are high. There are ways you can recover from hitting the ball in the rough or into a bunker. But there's no way to recover from a missed three-footer. It's a stroke lost. On the PGA Tour, this affects your livelihood. At your club, it may affect only your pride and a $2 bet, but the miss can still mean a lot to you. When the stakes are high, it's hard to dispel expectations and anxiety. They emanate from the conscious brain, and the overriding requirement of a good mental approach to putting is that you go unconscious.

That's why, for instance, many touring pros will tell you that they'd rather have a 12-foot putt to win a tournament than a three-foot putt. With the 12-footer, expectations are low. It's easier to follow the normal routine and go unconscious. When a pro faces a three-footer, though, he and everyone watching expect him to make it. It's much harder to go unconscious.

I recommended that Angel stop spending so much time on the practice putting green. I told him five to ten minutes a day would be enough, instead of the hours he'd been spending. I told him he would be better off away from the course, cooking up dinner (because he loves to cook), either not thinking about golf or thinking about putting great. A lot of professionals practice putting so much that they wind up placing additional pressure on themselves. Their putting deteriorates rather than improving.

Of course, Angel already knew how to putt. I also see amateurs who never practice putting because they don't want to put pressure on themselves. They never develop skills, either. There's a happy medium.

These days I hear and read an enormous amount of expertise on putting, much more than existed when I started counseling golfers. Then there are the new putters, the belly putters and the long putters. There are new ways to grip them. Putting options have proliferated. Not coincidentally, so have doubts.

A lot of the putting talk is confusing. Players and teachers talk, for instance, about "releasing" the putter. But they don't all mean the same thing when they use the term "release." Some want you to release the putter up, some over, and some around the line of the putt. Someone else will tell you release is just returning to your address position. Some experts will tell you that the putter blade needs to go straight up and down the target line. Others will tell you it should go inside, then along the line, then inside again.

All of these methods, all of these putters, and all of these grips can work. So can methods that no expert would ever recommend. I've seen players win tournaments coming across the line of the putt. They do it consistently and they have practiced it enough that it works for them. I have never advised a player that his putting style is hopeless, or that he needs to move the club with his shoulders rather than his hands, or switch putters or switch grips.

If one of my grandchildren, who are toddlers now, ever comes to me and asks me how to putt with the traditional style of putter, I'll suggest one alignment principle. I'll want his or her eyes over the ball or slightly inside the ball. This seems to help in aiming. Then I'll suggest envisioning the ball going to the hole or putting to a spot or putting to a picture. But I'll let the child pick the physical style. In my experience, golfers who have their eyes over the ball and who aim well tend to have a good stroke. It's instinctive. If your eyes are over the ball and your hands are hanging under your shoulders, your stroke is going to go back and forth.

While the putting style a player uses means little to me, I do care whether he himself believes in it. When I see a player arrive for a tournament with several different putters in his bag, I know I've got a problem to deal with. When a player who's constantly switching putters and grips and styles asks me to help him, one of the first things we work on is picking a method, believing in it, and sticking with it. **My experience is that a player can make almost any combination of style, grip, and equipment work if he believes in it.**

There is far less latitude on the mental side of putting. It is absolutely essential that a player sees the ball going into the hole and putts decisively. It is absolutely essential that a player has a sound, consistent putting routine. It is absolutely essential that a

player gets out of his own way and goes unconscious. People have various individual ways of doing these things. But all good putters, in my experience, share these traits.

Superficially, Keegan and Pat Bradley could not have more different putting styles. Pat uses a conventional putter, about halfway between a blade and a mallet. She grips it the same way she grips her clubs for longer shots, making sure to keep the handle in the creases of her fingers. She stands with her feet and hips square to the target line. It's a style she developed on her own, and she's comfortable with it.

Keegan watched his aunt Pat occasionally during her years on the LPGA Tour, when she won thirty-one tournaments and six majors. As Keegan got older, he and Pat played a lot of friendly rounds together. But Pat was wise enough not to push Keegan to copy her physical style with the putter. Keegan was wise enough to notice and try to emulate Pat's mental approach and will to win. He didn't try to copy her physical putting style. Keegan, as it happened, found that putting with a long putter anchored in his sternum felt very comfortable to him. So he adopted that style.

But while their physical putting styles are very different, Pat and Keegan share something that spectators and television cameras can't see.

When I started working with Pat, she had already been on the LPGA Tour for about a decade. She'd won ten tournaments, including a major. But she wanted more. She wanted to win multiple majors and make the LPGA Hall of Fame. Pat hit the ball an average distance off the tee for those years; her forte was a great chipping and pitching game. She was astute enough to realize that if she wanted to get more out of her talent, she had to improve her putting. But simply being aware of putting's importance had not helped her. In fact, as I watched her and worked with her, I could see that it had probably hurt her performance.

Pat worried so much about her putting that her routine got very fussy. She looked at the putt from behind the ball. She walked around and looked from behind the hole. She stopped halfway and tried to gauge the slope of the green from the side. She analyzed and reanalyzed. She thought she was doing her best by being so careful to read each putt correctly. In reality, she was making herself indecisive. She was fostering doubt.

I suggested to Pat that she revamp this phase of her routine. I encouraged her to go with her first impression, or instinct, about how a putt would break instead of trying to analyze the slope over and over. When I talk about following a golfer's instinct, or first read, on a golf course, I am really talking about letting the subconscious brain control the process.

When we first look at a ball and a green and a hole, our eyes transmit data to our brain. The brain, more often than not, responds with an "instinct" or "gut feeling" that comes partly from the subconscious. It's trying to tell us, "Hey, I remember one just like this. I know what it's going to do. Just put it on cruise control, buddy. I got this."

Pat had been putting her subconscious brain into conflict with her conscious brain. She was refusing to trust that gut feeling. Going with her first instinct helped make her calm and decisive.

She's not the only one. When I first started working with Tom Kite, we had some long discussions about this aspect of putting. His mother listened in. I can remember Mrs. Kite telling me that our conversation reminded her of Ben Crenshaw, who grew up playing with Tom. When he was a boy and a high school player, Mrs. Kite said, Ben never squatted down to read a green. He just walked onto the green, sizing up the slope as he walked, and hit the ball. He was enormously successful this way. As an adult, Ben started to read greens the way everyone else did. He was still a great putter, but in Mrs. Kite's eyes he was not quite the brilliant putter he had been as a boy.

When I suggest putting instinctively to clients, some accept the concept quickly. Others are skeptical. Maybe in their daily endeavors, they've found that "due diligence" pays off. They don't make a deal with someone because they like the way he shakes hands. They check out his credit report. They talk to advisers. They gather as much information as they can.

Due diligence has its place in business, but it doesn't work well in putting. If someone asks me, "Well, what if my first instinct is wrong?" I reply, "You're still better off putting decisively." Your first read will be correct more often than you might think. But you'll rarely sink an indecisive putt.

Once Pat Bradley agreed to go with her first read, she needed to channel her intensity in a way that would help her sink putts. I suggested visualization.

Putting is a very visual skill. Essentially, a good putter sees a target and his body reacts unconsciously to that target. **A golfer must reinforce that instinctive reaction by making an effort to visualize the ball going into the hole as she goes through her putting routine.** In fact, that's the only part of a pre-shot routine that really matters. It's the one constant I observe in all great putters.

People have different ways of visualizing. Some players tell me they see the ball going in as if they were watching a movie shot by a tiny camera atop the putter blade. They see the putter come down the line and strike the ball. They watch the ball roll, break, and fall in the hole. Some might see that process as well, but they see it from above, as if watching from a blimp. Other people don't see a rolling golf ball, but they see a line. Pat was one of these. She saw a line and she believed the ball would roll on that line. Her intensity was such that on short putts she felt that her mind was a laser, burning that line into the green, creating a path the ball had to follow.

Other golfers tell me they see parallel lines that look like railroad tracks, between which the ball will roll. Some see colored lines. Some see faint impressions in the grass. And some don't see lines at all. They see the path the ball will take.

Keegan Bradley didn't know about his aunt Pat's "laser" approach to putting until I mentioned it to him. He had already been impressed by the intensity he observed in her when he'd seen her play. After he won the PGA Championship in 2011, Keegan was asked about his memories of Aunt Pat as a tournament player. He recalled being impressed when he was a boy that she would walk right past him during a tournament round and not even recognize him. She was that impervious to distraction. When he heard about Aunt Pat's "laser vision," Keegan latched on to the idea of visualizing the line of a putt so that it felt like a laser was burning that line into the green. But where Pat saw the laser emanating from her mind, Keegan decided that his laser was going to come from each of his eyes. The beams would come together to burn his line to the hole. That's what he was seeing when he putted during the 2011 season, a season that saw him win his first tournament, the Byron Nelson, and his first major, the PGA.

Keegan has some other things in common with Aunt Pat, and I'm not thinking of their shared love for the Boston Red Sox. He putts to make it, something Pat always did. When I say "putt to make it," I mean that Keegan and Pat both would not putt until they had visualized the ball going into the hole. Once they'd done that, though, they simply reacted to the target and let whatever happened happen. I loved watching Keegan putt on the final hole of the playoff for the 2011 PGA. Even though he had only to two-putt the final green to win, Keegan stayed in his routine, and his routine calls for him to see the ball going in the hole and to react to his target. He rolled that last long putt fearlessly. It almost went in.

I recalled a conversation I'd had with Keegan and a young amateur player from Duke, Brinson Paolini, about eight months before the PGA. Keegan was just about to fly off to Hawaii for his first PGA Tour event. He wanted to talk, but I had a previous commitment to Brinson. So I invited both of them to dinner. Once we'd ordered, I asked Keegan to tell Brinson what he'd learned from our work together.

"Brinson," Keegan said, "I'll tell you what I've learned from Doc: to have more fun at golf, to let go of doubt, to let go of fear, and be into your target."

I had to smile at the memory as I saw Keegan hug his family and accept the Wanamaker Trophy. He had his own style, from his putter to his smile. But he and his aunt Pat shared the only important things about putting. They putted without fear and they putted to make it. Everything else is window dressing.

However a player does it, it's essential to feed the image of the ball going into the hole to the subconscious. It's essential that the golfer believes in it. This tells the brain what the body is supposed to do. Once you've envisioned the ball going into the hole, you're ready to putt and you need to step up and do it expeditiously, in accordance with your routine.

This principle makes some golfers nervous. "How will I know how hard to hit it?" they ask. "When I have a long putt, I'm worried about getting the speed right more than I am about getting the line right."

There's a misconception behind this question. It's the notion that there's only one correct speed for making a given putt. In fact, there are a lot of speeds at which a given putt can be made. If you don't understand this principle, try a practice drill my friend Brad Faxon showed me. Brad would pick a spot on a section of the practice green with a bit of slope to it. He'd put three balls down about six feet from the hole. And he would putt those three balls into the hole using three different lines and three different speeds. When he hit the putt firmly, he played less break. When he hit it at medium speed, he played more break. And when he hit the ball so it barely made it to the hole, he played still more break, so that the putt curled and fell in the side door.

This is a wonderful drill for improving your putting touch and imagination. I introduce it here to make the point that when your brain shows you a line, it's already figuring a speed into the equation. If you've been playing golf for any significant length of time, your brain has already observed this relationship between the speed of the putt and the amount it will break. It will, if you let it, give you an appropriate mix of speed and line.

This means that when a golfer is playing unconsciously, he looks at the ball, he looks at the green, and he looks at the hole. He visualizes the putt he wants. His brain automatically recognizes whether the putt is uphill or downhill. The brain quite accurately gauges the distance. The player doesn't have to tell himself to hit it easy or hit it hard. He doesn't have to worry about leaving it short or running it by. He just has to let the brain work unconsciously and let the putt happen.

Now, if a golfer is playing a course with very fast greens and he's got a downhill putt, it may well be advisable to putt the ball so it barely makes it to the hole and plops in just as it dies. Your brain will figure this out. It won't envision ramming the ball into the back of the cup on a downhill putt. Conversely, it will envision a firm putt if you're going uphill. Your brain is going to do this for you based on your past golf experience. The mistake would be letting the conscious brain override the subconscious's suggestion. Thoughts like *Don't run it past* or *Get it there this time, Alice* emanate from the conscious brain. Trust your subconscious brain.

I realize that trusting the subconscious this way requires some faith. So do some of the major steps people take in life. How does someone get married, pledge to be with one person forever, without trust and faith? But people do it. Golf may even be a little harder than marriage in that respect. A golfer must find a way to trust that the ball will go into the hole even when he's seen lots of his putts miss. It's not easy. But good players manage to do it.

There's a slightly misleading term floating around in golf that suggests that a player can "will" the ball into the hole. This leads some players to grit their teeth, hold the putter so hard their knuckles whiten, and try to make brain waves that will somehow propel the ball into the hole. That's not what willing the ball into the hole means to me. It should mean that the player commits to a line, visualizes the ball going into the hole along that line, trusts that it will go into the hole, and makes an unconscious stroke. There are no gritted teeth. There are no white knuckles.

This is perhaps better understood as "making the putt in your mind." If you've made the putt in your mind, you've done all that you can do. I know some very good players who build their rounds around this idea. Their goal is to make all their putts (and all their shots, for that matter) in their minds. If they do that, they're happy and satisfied, no matter how many of the putts actually dropped.

By the way, I have never understood the rationale for two old-fashioned putting principles, the three-foot target and the "green-light putt." It used to be that some professionals would tell pupils that on long putts, they should just aim to get the ball into a three-foot circle around the hole. But why? Sure, it's all right if a long putt winds up in a three-foot circle. But if you aim for a three-foot circle and miss by two feet, you're five feet away on your next putt. If you aim for the hole and miss by two feet, you've got a routine two-footer. Which would you rather have? What would you think of a basketball player who took a three-point shot with the backboard as his target instead of the basket?

Similarly, I don't get it when a television commentator looks at a player's putt and pronounces it a "green-light special" or says, "This is a putt he can try to make." Generally, I think, this is a label applied to uphill putts, on the theory that if you don't get the speed right on an uphill putt, your ball won't stop too far from the hole, but on a downhill putt you have to be primarily concerned with the possibility that the ball will roll too far past if you miss. When I hear this, my assumption is that the announcer is in the booth, rather than out on the course competing, because he's afraid of downhill putts.

If a putt's not a "green-light special," the implication is that it's a red-light putt, which means you're not trying to make it. Why would you ever hit a putt hoping to miss? You can, if you like, hit your uphill putts firmly, imagining that they'll bang against the back of the cup. And you can hit your downhill putts with the idea that they'll die in the hole. But the putt you envision, no matter how far away you are or what the slope of the green is, should always be one that goes to the cup.

I've spoken already of the cadence that characterizes a good routine for any stroke. This includes putts. When a player has chosen a line, he needs to take a few physical steps to make sure that he addresses the ball correctly and is aimed the way he needs to be. He needs to grip the club. A player needs to practice these steps often enough to be able to do them unconsciously during his routine. It helps to be able to do them deliberately but efficiently. Any undue delay increases the likelihood of the conscious brain becoming active.

At the heart of the physical routine are three steps: look at the target, look at the ball, and let the stroke go. Good players are often almost metronomic in their rhythm at this stage. There's no delay between the last look, bringing the eyes back to the ball, and stroking the putt. They never freeze over the ball. Players who freeze are usually either entertaining doubts about their line or giving themselves a putting-mechanics refresher course. Neither one is conducive to getting the ball into the hole. The only time a good putter might freeze during his routine is when he's behind the ball, figuring out the line of the putt. Once in a while, he won't have a clear first impression and he'll need to study the green a little longer in order to decide on a line and commit to it. He won't address the ball until he has that clarity. But once he does, there are no delays.

This is, after all, your chance to make putting an athletic activity, a reaction sport. Sometimes golfers who have been successful in other sports tell me they find golf hard because they don't get to react to anything the way a quarterback reacts to a receiver breaking free or a batter reacts to a pitch. Now you can react, if you maintain the correct cadence in your routine. You react to the target.

The metronomic cadence can be useful as a way to help a golfer clear his mind when he's putting. Mark Wilson's putting routine involves picking out a target and visualizing the line. He sees that line as if he were looking at the track a ball makes in the morning dew when a golfer is in the first group out. He selects his small target. Then he counts in a cadence he finds comfortable, that helps him add rhythm and flow in his stroke:

One: last look at the target.

Two: eyes back to the ball.

Three: putter goes back.

Four: impact.

This cadence helps clear his mind of any thoughts about the mechanics of his putting stroke or the situation he's in.

It's always advisable, as Mark does, to pick the smallest target your eyes can see without squinting. Don't just use the hole as a target, for example; putt to a specific little scuff mark inside the cup.

Many players like to straighten out every putt. If the line they envision indicates eight inches of break to the left, they pick a blade of grass or a discoloration eight inches to the right of the hole; that becomes their target, and they putt to it. Some players use the line they envision as a target. They just get the ball rolling on that line. Any of these methods is fine if it leads to unconscious execution of the stroke.

As with all other shots, the final step in a putting routine has to be total acceptance of whatever happens to the ball. This shouldn't be hard to do. Full shots travel mostly through a consistent medium, the air. The only misfortune that can befall them during most of their journey is a sudden gust of wind. Barring that, a full shot depends almost entirely on the way the golfer struck it. But a putt rolls along the ground. It can be, and often is, influenced by all of the imperfections of that ground—tiny pebbles, old pitch marks, a patch of dead grass. In contrast to a full shot, a golfer has less control over what happens once the ball leaves his putter blade. So, logically, it should be easier for a golfer to accept whatever happens to a putt.

Good players understand this, and they understand that the ball doesn't have to go in to make a putt successful. They believe that if they made the putt in their minds and honored their process, it's a successful putt.

Many players, however, react illogically. They're so dependent on results that they get angry when they miss a putt. I suppose anger has some utility in a few sports. If you're playing tug-of-war, for instance, it might help you pull really hard if you get angry at the other team. But golf is not like tug-of-war. Golf requires a clear mind and patience. You're less likely to have either if you permit yourself to get angry at a missed putt. If you want to cling to the idea that results are important, I suggest you remember that a good process is the best way to achieve successful results.

In my experience, anger over missed putts is quite often a precursor to panic. Just as thunder follows lightning, a player who gets angry when he misses a putt usually starts getting very conscious of technique, which tends to make him miss more. That's followed by panic. I define panic as abandoning your commitments in the middle of a round and trying something different, even if it's something you haven't practiced. I've seen players change their ball positions, their grips, and their strokes in the middle of rounds. They'll start putting left-hand low or using the claw grip. They'll try moving the putter in an arc rather than straight up and down the lines. Or vice versa. I strongly suspect you'd see a certain number of professionals changing putters midway through their rounds if the rules permitted them to.

Good putters don't do this. They find it easier to accept the results of any putt because they've developed a strong self-image as a putter. Their acceptance hastens the day when their actual putting approaches the putts they see in their minds.

EIGHT

THE SCORING CLUBS

You'd be surprised how often a golf shot turns out
just the way you're thinking.

—Patty Berg

At the 2011 Sony Open in Hawaii, Mark Wilson was feeling rushed. Rain had postponed play earlier in the week. On Sunday, players had to play 36 holes, finishing their third rounds and turning around almost immediately to start their fourth. Mark, after shooting a 65 to take the 54-hole lead, barely had time to grab a dozen new golf balls and the chicken sandwich he keeps in his locker for an on-course protein infusion. He arrived on the first tee with about two minutes to spare. He felt like a high school kid rushing to grab his books and get to class on time.

This class opened with a pop quiz on the short game.

The first at Waialae is a 488-yard par four. The approach to the green is affected very much by the prevailing wind. Mark hit a 6-iron and thought he hit it well, but the ball came up just a little short; perhaps the wind died a little as the ball flew.

He left himself a very testing pitch shot. Like a lot of courses, Waialae had recently been revamped to make the green complexes more difficult. Mark's ball found one of those difficulties, coming to rest 30 feet from the hole but just a few inches to the right of a deep greenside bunker. He would have to take his stance in the sand, with the ball about even with his knees. Mark devotes the bulk of his practice time to shots from 120 yards and closer to the hole. But this was not a shot he'd ever really practiced. He would have to be creative and trust his skills.

He went through his short-game routine. He checked the lie, gauging how fluffy it was, how much it might slow his club head down, and how the ball would likely spin coming out of it. By this moment, after a week at Waialae, those calculations were instinctive. He envisioned the shot he wanted and its trajectory—a pitch of medium height that would land short of the hole and trickle into it. He took his stance and gripped down on the handle of his 60-degree wedge, down so far his left hand was touching steel instead of leather. "I tried to pretend I was really short," he said later. Knowing that he needed to ensure good contact, he pressed forward a little bit with his hands, tilting the handle of the club toward the target. Then he went unconscious, looked one last time at the target, brought his eyes back to the ball, and swung.

He got the contact he had imagined, clean and solid. The ball landed eight feet short of the hole, just about as he'd planned. But the ball came out a bit hotter than he'd expected. It missed the flagstick and rolled six feet past the hole.

That didn't fluster Mark. When he practices his short game, he tries always to putt the ball out. In his mind, the pitch is just part of a process that leads to getting the ball in the hole. A pitch is only an end in itself if he pitches it in. No matter how good a pitch is, it means little to Mark if he doesn't make the putt.

In this case, Mark rolled the six-footer into the hole, despite the pressure of having the lead and feeling rushed. The par, as he recalls, settled him down. He went on to shoot 67 and win by two strokes.

That's the power of a good short game. **A player who knows he can get up and down from anywhere, who can occasionally turn a missed green into a birdie by pitching the ball into the hole, has a tremendous advantage in golf.** Little bothers him. When he misses a green, he remains calm. A pitch or a bunker shot is no different to him than a long putt.

In fact, it's been my observation that all great putters are also great pitchers of the golf ball. Their pitching game gives them lots of short putts, putts they hole. The confidence that flows from those made putts improves their game on and around the greens. They feel less pressure with every club. They get happy every time they approach a green, regardless of where their ball happens to be. The green is their stage. It's where they excel.

That's one reason I believe it's a great idea for kids, or any beginning golfer, to learn the game from the hole outward—learning to putt, then hitting the little greenside shots, and only then learning the full swing. If a youngster realizes early on the centrality of the short game, he or she is more likely to learn it and value it. For that reason, since I've already talked about putting, I'm going to cover the mental approach to the rest of the scoring club shots from greenside pitches to approaches with the 8-iron, 9-iron, and wedges.

PITCHING

If I had to rank these shots in the order of their importance, I would say that **a good pitch shot is the most important wedge shot a golfer can have.** Almost inevitably, an excellent player will confront the need for a short pitch shot during the course of a round. An average player will have these shots many times a round. Occasionally, the player will have an alternative—putting or bumping a hybrid through a fairway opening to the green, for instance. But there are going to be times when there is no alternative to the pitch shot because the player has rough or a hazard between his ball and the green.

If you want to play golf at a high level, you need at least a couple of pitch shots in your repertoire. You need a shot with medium trajectory and backspin. You'll use that shot when you need to hit over a bunker and stop the ball near the hole. You'll use it if you're short of the green and the flag is on a tier at the top. A good player can pitch the ball to that tier and stop it. Good players will also learn to pitch the ball so it spins less and rolls out to the target.

You may be an average player who, reading this, thinks it's already tough for you to hit a plain pitch off a tight lie. You may think I'm asking a lot when I say you need at least two different pitch shots. I wouldn't argue with you. But if you want to move from being average to playing at a high level, to seeing how good you can get, you need to start developing this ability.

The second short-game shot you'll need is a bunker shot. I'll discuss it in a moment.

It used to be that the first wedge shot a player learned was the chip shot, and chipping was considered an essential skill. But that was back when course conditions were not nearly as good as they are now. The fairways of today resemble the greens that I grew up on. A player can putt from five feet off the green, perhaps farther on particularly well-kept courses. He can use his putting stroke to bump a hybrid or a fairway metal. So the chip shot has declined in importance. I'd place it third on my list of priorities, behind the pitch and the bunker shot.

The lob would be last on that list. I'm not saying that it isn't nice to have a good lob shot, by which I mean a pitch that goes very high, without much spin, and rolls very little. It stops near its landing spot because of its extreme trajectory. The lob has become fashionable, particularly since the advent of the 60-degree wedge. But I know Tour players who won't hit a lob off a tight lie in competition. They get along very nicely with a few pitch shots, and they can hit a lob from the rough. If you can reach the Tour level without a lob off a tight lie, I suspect you can do well enough without it at the club level.

Now you know the short-game shots you need and their relative importance. I'm not going to talk about the mechanics of hitting them. If you don't know the mechanics, you need to learn them from a good teacher. I'll discuss later on how to identify and cultivate a relationship with such a teacher. I'll also discuss what you need to do if you once knew the mechanics but have developed mental problems with these clubs that cripple your game—the so-called yips. But I will tell you now that from a physical standpoint, these greenside wedge shots are simpler than the shots you hit with a full swing. The clubs are shorter. The swings are shorter. There are fewer movements to coordinate.

I've already described how tossing a ball, or even a book, across a room to a target demands roughly the same amount of physical talent as pitching a golf ball. Of course, I have a lot of clients who can toss the ball into my hand but can't hit a pitch shot or a bunker shot under pressure. They may think this is because it's hard to hit a pitch shot. In reality, it's because they're getting in their own way.

I understand why. If the average amateur hits a good tee shot, then misses the green by 20 feet with a long iron, she's playing up to her physical abilities, or close to them. She's thinking that it would be great to get a par and at the very least she should make bogey. With this thought, the conscious brain takes over control. The next thought is very likely, *On the other hand, if I skull this pitch or chunk it, I could easily turn this hole into a double bogey and waste those two good shots.* That might be followed with, *I'll be so embarrassed if that happens because it looks like this should be an easy shot.* And if this golfer has been playing for a while, that thought might be followed with, *Gee. I skulled a shot something like this last year in the member-guest. I'll never forget that.*

If this describes your mental process as you walk toward a pitch shot, it might be some consolation to you to know that you're not alone. As I've mentioned, quite a few players in the U.S. Open of 2011 had some doubt and fear about pitching the ball at Congressional. Not many amateurs like hitting short pitches off tight lies. Their true game plan is to make their way around the course avoiding them. I see lots of players who will aim for the left edge of a green and take their chances on winding up in a bunker if the right side drops away to a tightly-mowed area requiring a deft pitch. If they nevertheless wind up in that situation, I'll see them putt the ball from as much as 25 feet off the green.

I would never argue with that decision. If a top Tour player was feeling insecure about a pitch, in competition, he'd back off and putt it. He wouldn't care if he putted from 25 yards off the green, let alone 25 feet. (If he were my client, of course, and he wanted to remain on the Tour, we'd soon be having a serious talk about what he needed to do to be able to pitch the ball confidently in that situation.) But I tell players that in competition, I want them to hit whatever club and whatever shot they can envision themselves hitting well. The only relevant question in competition is "How am I going to hit it closest or hit it in the hole?"

The answer to that question might not be the same every day. **A player must be honest with himself. If he can't manage a clear mind about a given shot and he has an alternative that will give him a clear mind, he needs to hit the alternative.**

Similarly, I never prescribe to a client the trajectory or the club he should select. It's too personal. If I am walking along during a practice round with a Tour player and he asks, "What would you hit in this situation?" I always answer, "Why would you care? I'm going to hit the one I can see and I want you to hit the one you can see."

One of the beauties of the short game is that it's your game and no one else's. Some great players like to use their imaginations to figure out how the ball will respond to the bumps and slopes in the ground. They hit low pitches and get them running on the ground as soon as they can. Others revel in the look and feel of a high pitch that comes down near the hole, bounces once, and then checks and stops. Some people like to use one club for all their pitch shots; they vary their trajectories by changing ball position, opening the club face or closing it down. Others like to match their envisioned trajectories to different clubs and make basically the same swing each time. My attitude toward the different pitching styles brings to mind something Chinese leader Deng Xiaoping once said. The color of the cat doesn't matter, according to Deng, as long as it catches mice. He was talking about economic systems, but it applies equally well to short-game techniques. **The only pertinent question is "Does it get the ball into or very close to the hole?"**

I do, however, add one caveat to that general rule. No matter what your preferred style in pitching the ball, you have to strive to make it easy, effortless, trusting, and unconscious. The more complex your short game is, the more work it's going to take to go unconscious. **So if you're a weekend player with limited time to practice, it's worth considering simplifying your approach. Maybe you'll want to just use one setup and one ball position, or one pitching club and one ball position, varying only the degree to which you open the club face.**

It's fine to experiment with different techniques while you're in the learning phase. But well before it's time to compete, you need to come to closure on a pitching technique that feels right to you. Then stick with it. Today, I read and hear a lot more debate about the best way to pitch the ball than I heard a couple of decades ago. A lot of players who have been good pitchers of the ball hear about something someone else is doing, and they decide to try that. Then they start bouncing back and forth between techniques, and pretty soon they're lost. Don't be one of those players. Work with a teacher, decide on a technique, and stick with it.

If at some point thereafter you find that your short game isn't working, the likelihood is that it's not your pitching technique that's flawed. It's your execution of the technique. When I work with a player who's constantly trying new short-game techniques, I sometimes want to ask what he would do if his business had a bad quarter. Would he abandon his business plan, fire his employees, and start over? Or would he figure out where he and his staff were failing to execute their plan? If most golfers paid attention to proper execution of their short-game techniques and routines, rather than looking for new ones, they'd be better off.

You will need a specific pitching routine. As with any short-game shot, the first thing you'll be doing is assessing your situation and picking a target. What kind of lie do you have? What kind of terrain lies between you and the hole? What are the hazards? How will the ball roll once it hits the green? Your lie is going to affect your choice of shots and targets. There are lies near a green where the ball sits up, clean contact is possible, and a good player can pitch the ball to virtually any target. In those cases, the target should be the hole. There may be other situations, like a pitch from a terrible lie in the rough over a bunker to a pin on the short side of the green, where even the best players are going to decide that their target is the middle of the green.

Once you've decided on a target, if you're in the rough, you might, like Mark Wilson, take a practice swing or two to feel how this particular patch of long grass will affect the club head as you swing through it. You may also need to take a stance very close to your eventual address location and decide how the slope of the ground will affect the shot. You don't want to take your real stance and begin the heart of your routine, then be interrupted with a thought like, *This slope is much steeper than I anticipated!*

If you're just playing casually, your calculations about the lie and the target may be different from those you'd make in a tournament. When a player is out by himself in the twilight, for instance, he ought to try to get close to any hole from any lie, just to see if he can. But if he's in a competition, I suggest that a player apply the 80 percent rule.

Suppose, for instance, that your second shot on a par five winds up in the fairway forty yards short of the green, and the green is just beyond a pond. On this particular day, the hole is cut only a couple of paces from the edge of the pond. You could try to land the ball just over the pond and stop it by the hole, leaving a short birdie putt. Or you could aim for a landing spot in the middle of the green, leaving a long birdie putt but taking the pond out of play.

Your strategy will depend on your assessment of your skills. If you feel that you'll pull the shot off eight times out of ten, try landing the ball just over the water and stopping it close to the hole. If you feel you'll miss that shot more than 20 percent of the time, pick the target in the middle of the green. Regardless of which strategy you choose, of course, you need to have a clear mind in order to give yourself the best possible chance to hit the shot successfully.

However, I'll be clear here. Good players, by definition, make the hole their target on the vast majority of their short pitches. If you want to become a good player, you need to develop your short game to the point where you can, too.

Good players always put envisioning the shot at the center of their routines. As with putting, players have different ways of imagining the shot they want to hit. Some will see everything the ball is going to do: its trajectory, its landing spot, its roll into the hole (assuming the hole is the target). Others will see only the trajectory and the landing spot. Others may see only the hole, the ball's ultimate destination, and simply believe that the ball is going there. It doesn't matter as long as you see it and commit to it.

As I've mentioned, good players frequently incorporate more practice swings into their pitching routines than they do for other shots. But once they're ready to go, their routines acquire the same sort of unconscious grace that characterizes the routines they use for putting and other shots. Their minds go blank, or as close to unconscious as they can get them. They dispel all mechanical thoughts, all doubts, all fears.

Sometimes a client will listen to this description of the pitching routine and say, "What if I can't get my mind clear? What if I can't get confident? I still have to hit the pitch shot in certain situations."

In those cases, I tell the client that the inability to feel confident about a shot means he's not ready for competition, at least not at a high level. He has to do the best he can, even if the best shot he can hit at the moment may not be very good at all. It happens.

The important thing is to learn from it. If you find yourself out on the golf course competing and unable to be confident about pitches, it means you have work to do. I'll discuss a little farther on the mental steps a player can take to repair a short game that's been undermined by doubt or fear. I'll discuss practice games and drills that all players can use to sharpen their short games and enable themselves to go unconscious. One way or another, you have to decide you're eventually going to reach that level.

Just as with putting, or any other shot, the ideal pitch routine has a distinct rhythm to it. Once you've identified your target, envisioned your shot, taken your practice swings, and addressed the ball, get on with it. Don't rush, but don't tarry, either. When golfers stop for a long time during their routine, they tend to get conscious, to get tight, to get careful. Look at the target. Look at the ball. Let it go.

Finally, you have to accept the result of the shot, whatever it is. I've spoken about the importance of endowing every shot with the same low level of importance, regardless of whether it's in the last few holes of a tournament or the second hole of a Tuesday practice round. When a player does that, he avoids overreacting to any shot, particularly the ones that don't work out the way he'd hoped they would.

Keegan Bradley displayed this skill to the world when he won the 2011 PGA Championship. Keegan got a tough bounce when he hit his tee shot to the 15th hole in the final round. I thought the ball would kick onto the green, close to the hole. Instead, it bounced into a terrible lie in deep, thick rough. The world saw Keegan's next shot, a pitch, come out of the grass lower and hotter than he expected, then roll into the water.

Many players would have let that shot ruin their tournament. But Keegan accepted it, went to the drop zone, and cleared his mind. His subsequent birdies on the 16th and 17th holes, his gutsy shots on the difficult 18th, and his ultimate triumph in the playoff showed his mental discipline.

The opposite reaction is panic. After an unsuccessful shot, I see players renege on their commitment to a pitching technique. They change their ball position or the angle of the club shaft. Their conscious minds go wild, and they remember all the lessons and tips they've had or heard about and they try to alter and control the next swing. It doesn't work.

If you hit a poor pitch shot and your mind was clear, it's likely that you didn't do something you thought you were doing. Rather than try a different technique, stick with the technique and routine you've committed to, the one you've practiced. If your mind wasn't clear, do your best to go unconscious on the next shot.

BUNKER PLAY

As I've said, the professionals I work with often find it much easier to go unconscious when their ball is in a bunker than they do when it's on a tight lie in the grass. That's partly because they don't actually hit the ball when they hit an explosion shot. It seems easy to them. But I know that many amateurs find it hard to believe when they watch a tournament on television and hear a player mutter, "Get in the bunker," as he watches a wayward shot approach a green. To many amateurs, the bunker is truly a trap, a scary place to be. They can't believe that a pro would rather be in the sand than in thick rough or pitching off a closely mowed slope.

In order to begin to share a pro's confidence in the bunker, you're going to have to understand how your wedge is supposed to work in the bunker, sliding under the ball but not touching it, lifting the ball out in an explosion of sand. If you've played much golf, you know this.

But I still have a lot of clients who worry about it. They're afraid they're going to hit the ball as well as the sand and that fear paralyzes them.

Most of them have a combination of mechanical issues. They may not be opening the club face up, using the club head's bounce correctly, or setting up so they know they'll contact sand first as they swing. If you suspect your bunker technique is deficient in one or more of these ways, you need to find a teacher to work on corrections with you.

There are degrees of sophistication in bunker play. When I give a clinic for high handicappers, I often find them scared to death of bunker shots. I try to start them off hitting pitch shots from the rough, then, when they can do that, move them into a bunker. I suggest that they use the same swing in the bunker that they used for their pitch shots, only making sure they contact the sand before they hit the ball. Nearly always, these high handicappers find that they can at least get the ball out of the bunker on a consistent basis. They can't always get it close to the hole, but their fear of bunker shots fades away. If they tell me they want to do better than merely get the ball out of the sand, that they want to be able to get the ball up and down from a bunker, I suggest that they begin by taking a lesson or two from a good teacher on bunker play.

Once you've got a bunker swing that will hit the sand consistently and you're using the club correctly, you'll need a good bunker routine. It's much like the pitch shot routine except that you do much of it outside the bunker. You visualize the shot outside the bunker. You select your target outside the bunker. You take your practice swings outside the bunker. You commit to the shot you've seen and the swing you've rehearsed.

Let's suppose, for instance, that you were in the back bunker behind the 18th green at the Bay Hill Club and Lodge in Florida, the site of Arnold Palmer's PGA Tour event every March. The green slopes away from this bunker, and beyond it is a pond. The hole is always cut close to the pond for the final round of the tournament.

A player without mental discipline might be paralyzed by fear of hitting the ball instead of the sand and seeing the ball fly into the water, so much so that he reacts by hitting too far behind the ball and leaving it in the bunker. When a good player, one who has mental discipline, envisions this shot, he's looking for a way to get the ball in the hole, but he's also cognizant that if he hits it long, it's wet. So instead of envisioning a bunker shot that flies nearly to the hole, checks up, and plops in, he envisions a shot that lands 15 feet short of the hole, with less spin, and then trickles down to the hole and in. Only when that image is firm in his mind does he step into the bunker.

Once in a while, you may have to stop and restart your bunker routine. If, for instance, you walk into a bunker on a golf course that's new to you, and you realize the sand doesn't have the consistency you expected, I suggest you stop, walk out, put your club back into the bag, and start the process over again. You may need to switch to a wedge with a different bounce angle to better match the sand texture you sensed with your feet—more bounce for softer sand, less bounce for firm sand.

Once all that is taken care of, though, the bunker routine is exactly like your routine for any shot. You look at the target, look back to the ball, and without conscious thought, let the swing go. Padraig Harrington tells me that this is essentially what he practices when he practices bunker shots. He works on getting into his target and letting the stroke go unconsciously. In the last two years he's become one of pro golf's best bunker players.

APPROACH SHOTS WITH SHORT IRONS

The length of a short-iron approach shot varies greatly with the skill of the player involved, but the importance does not. Success with these short-game shots is critical to any player's score. For a professional, it's imperative to hit approaches with short irons (the 8-iron and 9-iron) not only on the green but close to the hole. At the other end of the spectrum, high handicappers, particularly as they age, often can't get to a par four in two shots. They consistently have pitches of forty to sixty yards to reach the green with their third shot. If they play those shots skillfully, they can shoot in the 70s and 80s. If they play them poorly, they have difficulty breaking 100.

The Tour pros I work with devote time and attention to honing their skills with these clubs. A lot of them nowadays use a device that tracks exactly how far a shot travels in the air and gives them instant feedback. They want to know how far a "normal" 9-iron flies, how far a "crushed" 9-iron will go, and how far an "easy" 9-iron will go. The machine tells them. Other pros have their caddies stand a certain distance away from the practice tee to get a reading.

I understand that most amateurs don't have caddies or the wherewithal to invest in one of these devices. They don't have to. You can put towels down on the practice range and use a range-finder to figure out how far your shots are carrying. At Oklahoma State, one of the nation's best college programs, the players don't hit buckets of balls and there is no tractor on the practice range with an attachment to pick up balls. Players practice from their own ball bags and when they're done, they pick up their own balls. They learn quickly how far they hit the ball with each club.

A player must know that in order to be confident enough to make the hole his target with a short iron. It doesn't matter if it's a professional's 165-yard 8-iron or a club player's 50-yard lob wedge. Precision is important, and it's one of the highest practice priorities of good players.

Players sometimes ask me what they should do about "awkward" distances. I know good college golfers, for example, who play well in close proximity to the green but get tense, conscious, and awkward at half-swing distances from 20 yards to 100 yards. Farther than that, they can take full swings with their irons, and their confidence returns. I tell them that there's nothing wrong with laying up to a favorite distance on short par fours and long par fives. At the same time, I add, if the college player wants to help his team and win, he's going to have to develop skills at all of those intermediate distances. They should be his highest priority in practice.

Sometimes, the target for your lay-up will vary with the way the green is set up. Suppose you have a par five with the pin set at the back of the green. You might want to lay up close to the green but in the rough, so your pitch shot will have no spin and roll up to the hole. You might want to lay up to a full-swing distance in the fairway if the pin is set close to the front, so your pitch will have maximum backspin.

Average players sometimes ask me about "in-between distances." If your 9-iron goes 120 yards and your 8-iron goes 130, what should you hit when the flag is 125 yards away? Is it better to hit the 9 hard or the 8 easy? My answer is neither. Both require conscious thought that could affect your grace, rhythm, and coordination. It's better, if you're an average player, to pick the club that will get you closer to the middle of the green. Make that your target, then swing unconsciously.

The routine for short-irons is almost identical to the routine for pitching. The player needs to identify his target, envision his shot, let himself go, and then unconsciously react to his target. Use your first instinct on club selection. If the course requires a tough approach shot, your routine is your ally. Many of my clients win when they're telling themselves, ***Okay, I've seen it and I know where it's going and no matter where it ends up, I am going to accept it, go get it, and score with it. Now that I know this, let's just do the routine.*** **They don't win when they're telling themselves,** ***I've got to pure this. I've got to get it close.***

Some of you may have read to this point and be thinking, *All right, Rotella. I just wish my bad thoughts were* I've got to get this close. *I can't look at a pitch shot without thinking of disaster. I can try to swing unconsciously, but all I can do is twitch at the ball and chunk it or skull it. My short game is an utter wreck and it's making me want to quit golf. What can I do?*

Read on.

NINE

FIXING A WRECKED SHORT GAME

You defeat defeatism with confidence.

—Vince Lombardi

I see them often when I play golf for fun: players with wrecked short games. They're men and women who can hit their tee shots and their irons. But when they miss a green, they're in trouble. They're the people who try to putt the ball out of bunkers, even when the trap has a lip. They'll putt the ball out of the rough, from as many as 15 yards from the green. When they absolutely have to hit a pitch shot or a bunker shot, it's as if an anguished face is the first step in their pre-shot routines. I don't have to read minds to know that they're envisioning disaster. The coordination they display on the tee vanishes. The ensuing shots are predictably ugly. Sometimes, skulled, they skitter across the green and into a tough spot on the other side. Sometimes, chunked, they barely move.

I don't see problems quite this dramatic when I work with professionals, but I do see a surprising number of players who are afraid of certain greenside shots, especially under tournament pressure. There are pros who, faced with a shot off a tight lie to get the ball close to a front hole location, will put the ball back in their stance and punch a little chip 15 feet past, because at least they know they'll make clean contact. Instead of being into their targets, they bail out due to fear and doubt. That's the best they can do under pressure.

These players, whether pro or amateur, most likely once had short games on the same level as their full-swing games. But something has happened to them. A lot of them like to tell me they have somehow caught a case of the "chip yips."

Now, I have seen a lot of players with wrecked short games, but I have yet to see convincing scientific evidence for the existence of a physical condition called "the yips." I know that there are some institutions that claim to have identified this supposed malady of the nervous system; but since they also tend to be places that are in the business of treating it as a medical problem, I am not surprised.

There are no doubt golfers who play despite tremors or other issues caused by real diseases. I admire them. But in 99 percent of the "yips" cases I have seen, the player who thinks he has the yips doesn't have a disease. He may have a problem with short putts but not with long putts. He may pitch the ball well in practice but not in competition. If such a player truly had a medical condition, he would have as much trouble with long putts as with short putts. He would pitch the ball as poorly on the practice ground as on the golf course.

This is why golfers who switch grips, or switch to long putters, instantly cure their yips. If they had a physical affliction, it would show up regardless of the putter they used. It's a little different with the short wedge shots around the green. There, I've seen combinations of mental and technique problems. But I've still never seen a nervous affliction that forces a player to hit bad wedge shots.

In my experience, short-game problems often begin with a single, traumatic shot that leads to a combination of mental and mechanical issues. A typical example is Marty Jacobson, my friend with the brisk routine. Marty has been a fine player for many years. He isn't long, but he hits a little draw down the middle all day, and his handicap has been in the single digits since he was a kid. He's always loved to compete.

A few years ago, Marty was in a playoff in a member-guest at Elk River in North Carolina. The format was alternate shot, which can be stressful; an amateur who forms the guest half of the member-guest team often feels extra pressure because he likes the player who invited him and doesn't want to let him down. Marty is normally very good at visualizing the shot he wants to hit, but on the third playoff hole, he faced a chip shot. Marty couldn't keep negative thoughts from swirling through his mind. Everyone in the field was following the playoff contestants in golf carts. The lie was tight. It was a stressful situation. Marty skulled the chip over the green.

That began a rough patch for Marty's short game. I've seen worse. A skulled chip in that sort of situation can haunt a player. It sears itself into his memory because he invested such emotion in it; it was not just for himself but for his friend. After that kind of shot, a lot of players have trouble clearing their minds, visualizing the shot they want, and going unconscious.

Marty had always been good at visualizing his shots before he hit them, but for a while he couldn't visualize good results. He'd see himself hitting fat shots or thin ones. His conscious mind flooded his brain with pre-shot advice like *Don't decelerate.* He rushed through his routine, trying to get the shot over with. His particular nemesis was the 10- to 15-yard shot from a tight lie.

Players in this predicament usually tighten up. They get obsessed with results instead of process. They tell themselves they have a short-game problem instead of a problem with the way they think. This leads to mechanical issues. Fear prevents them from moving as fluidly and gracefully as they do when they hit full shots with the driver. Contact is inconsistent. They often either hit the ground behind the ball or flip the club with their wrists and hands, trying to avoid hitting it fat. That results in skulled shots. Even when they manage to make good contact, they don't get the ball particularly close to their targets. Why would they? The target was the last thing on their minds when they addressed the ball. They were worried about contact.

If this reminds you of yourself, you have work to do. But the problem is soluble.

The first step is an honest self-assessment. Is your problem only a mental problem? Or is it a combination of mental and mechanical issues, each side feeding off the other until you hate and fear the short game?

One indicator would be whether you can pitch and chip the ball very well at the practice green but can't do it on the course, in competition. That would suggest your problem lies mainly in your mind. I find this to be the case with many of the professionals who come to me with short-game issues. With amateurs, I sometimes see players who make poor, twitchy swings when there's a ball involved but make graceful swings that nip the grass when there's no ball and they're taking practice swings. Whether they're pros or amateurs, they can make good swings with their scoring clubs. They're getting in their own way mentally. We'll call this problem Scenario One.

On the other hand, there are players who can't hit good chips and pitches when they're out by themselves in their club's short-game practice area with a bag full of balls. They can't make good practice swings. This suggests a combination of mechanical and mental flaws. We'll call this problem Scenario Two.

One way to find out if your case is Scenario One or Scenario Two is to try a diagnostic game I sometimes play with a client. Get a two-by-six board and some practice balls. Have a friend roll the balls, one at a time, down the board so they roll toward you. Take your address position with a wedge in your hands. As each ball comes to you, try to hit a nice, high pitch shot with it.

Most golfers, to their surprise, can almost immediately start hitting pretty good pitch shots in this setting. It's because they have to react to the moving ball. They have no time to worry about how to do it. They have no time to worry about what their shot is going to look like. They have no expectations for the results of the shot and there are no consequences if they miss one. Given those factors, they're fine. They've shown themselves that if they could clear their minds, they would have no mechanical issues that would prevent them from having a good short game. They fit Scenario One.

On the other hand, if you tried to hit pitch shots with your head totally clear and couldn't do it, that would indicate Scenario Two, the combination of mental and mechanical problems. I know this is a book about the mental side of the short game, but if your short-game problems resemble Scenario Two, I'm not going to pretend that they can be solved only by changing your thinking. **If basic mechanical flaws have affected your short game, you need to fix them. You need to go on a mission to learn how to pitch the ball. You have to approach this mission with patience. You can't expect to succeed immediately. But you can accelerate the process by finding a good teacher.**

Most any golf professional will agree to give you a short-game lesson, but that doesn't make every golf professional a good short-game teacher. Some pros are much more comfortable teaching the full swing. Before you pick a teacher, ask around. Find some friends who have taken short-game lessons from him or her, particularly people who have worked on the same issue you have. Was the pro enthusiastic about teaching the short game? Was he effective?

Before you take a lesson, talk to the teacher you're considering. Ask her how she teaches the short game. What you're looking for here is a combination of things. Does the instructor sound like she really loves teaching the short game? And is she flexible? By that I mean, does she have one way of presenting the short game that she uses with every pupil? Or is she the sort of teacher who will try lots of different ways to present the same idea, because she knows that people learn in different ways? A teacher might, for example, tell a pupil to keep his weight on his left foot. And that will help many students. But others will feel off balance, and they'll get tense if they're thinking about keeping their weight on their left foot. A good teacher will try a different approach with this kind of pupil. She might tell him to turn the buttons on his shirt past the target line. And this will feel very different to the pupil from keeping his weight on his left foot. In reality, the two approaches wouldn't look very different to an outsider. They'd both lead to the pupil having his weight where it needed to be when he struck the ball. But one approach would work for this particular individual and one wouldn't. There are many paths that lead to the destination, and a good teacher recognizes this.

Understand that you own your instruction. If you were an athlete in high school or college, you didn't get to pick your coach; the school picked him for you. And there were some advantages to that. You totally agreed with what the coach told you and you did your best to execute it. (Or you weren't on the team.) It was a lot easier to believe what you were told, because there were no options. But now you're selecting the teacher and paying him to teach you, and there are a lot of competing sources of advice and instruction. On the one hand, you owe it to your teacher to be dedicated and committed. This will very likely improve the quality of your instruction. Teachers are only human. If the teacher knows you're going to do your best to implement and practice his suggestions, he's very likely going to work harder for you.

On the other hand, you have the responsibility to decide when a teacher just isn't helping you. This isn't an easy decision to make, but sometimes it's necessary. Maybe the teacher is suggesting methods that you're certain will never feel right to you, even though they might work for other people. Maybe he insists on presenting his ideas in ways that just don't work with your learning style. If you're certain that you've given a teacher a fair chance and that you've practiced diligently, and things are still not improving, sometimes the best thing to do is to part company.

Let's assume you've found a good teacher and are on the way

to fixing your mechanical problems. Learning the correct mechanics will take some time and practice. My friend Bob Christina, the motor-skills learning specialist, tells me that it's very difficult to predict precisely how much time and physical practice will be needed for an individual to develop the neural networks that will allow him to repeat a proficient swing unconsciously, especially under the pressure of competition. But it certainly won't happen instantly.

At some stage in this process, however, you're going to need some closure. **You're going to need to make up your mind that you now know a solid technique, one that works for you. And you're going to have to say, "Okay, for the rest of my life, this is the way I want to hit pitch shots." Or bunker shots, or chips, or whatever your problem has been.**

Now, under Scenario Two, you've addressed your mechanical issues. You're next going to have to address your thinking about the short game. You're at roughly the same place as players whose short-game issues resemble Scenario One. In either case, you have to construct a new attitude.

I say "construct" because this is a building process. There won't be a light switch you can flip to solve your mental issues instantly, any more than you could solve your mechanical issues instantly.

You begin by making a conscious effort to throw away the past, particularly the past mistakes you have made in wedge play. Sometimes a golfer will tell me this isn't "realistic," because what happened in the past is real, it's part of his history.

I hear much the same thing from athletes in other sports, such as basketball players. When a basketball player tells me this, I have a simple answer. I have him sit down and watch a tape of one of Michael Jordan's games with the Chicago Bulls, back when Jordan was in his prime. I have the player make a note of every Jordan "mistake," whether it's a missed shot, a basket scored by the opponent he was guarding, or a turnover. The list of Jordan's "mistakes" fairly quickly fills up a page or two.

So, I ask, was it "realistic" of Michael Jordan to remain a supremely confident player, one who wanted and expected to have the ball in his hands when the game was on the line? Of course it was. Jordan chose to remember his good shots and to forget his mistakes.

There are ways to assist yourself in doing this. Change the way you watch televised golf. Make a note of all the shots your favorite player hits imperfectly. Notice how he responds. Most people are very good at remembering their own bad shots, and they're very good at remembering another player's good shots. Be the opposite. Forget your own bad shots. Remember the bad shots of other players, and notice how they don't let those bad shots ruin their rounds.

Reinforce the memory of your good shots. Some people find reinforcement if they write things down. For them, I recommend a journal. If wedge shots are the ones that have been giving you trouble, get into the habit of writing down a phrase or a sentence describing the fine wedge shots you make, even if they're only in practice. After every round you play, write a brief description of every time you missed a green but got up and down. This will help you relive and strengthen the memories you want to keep.

If you're not the writing sort, you can use video technology and a friend to give you a visual reinforcement for good memory. Have a friend make a videotape of you hitting some excellent wedge shots. Loop it so it plays over and over again. Watch it often. I suggest a variant on this to Tour pros. They can have someone tape their best shots from tournament telecasts. Then, at home, they can watch their own highlights show.

This may strike you as odd or egocentric. All I can say in response is that it works. If you don't want to write or use video, then set aside some quiet time after each round you play and each practice session. Reflect on each good shot you made, particularly the short-game shots. Take control of your memory.

You should also start talking to someone about your successes. If you've been a poor short-game player for a while, you've had a long stretch of bad thoughts and memories. You've berated yourself. You've visualized a lot of mistakes before they happen. Then you've relived a lot of bad shots. You need to start doing the opposite. One of my functions when I counsel a player with short-game problems is serving as a listener. I give the player permission, in the broadest sense, to brag about his accomplishments. I want him to call me about the good shots he's made. Your teacher can and should serve this function for you. Your playing partners may not want to sit in the bar after the round and listen to you brag about the good shots you made. But you need to find someone who will.

Visualization is a major component in this effort, just as it should be in your overall approach to golf. **Develop the habit of seeing yourself getting up and down from bunkers, from tight lies, from anyplace else that has given you trouble in the past.** Set aside some time for visualization each day, perhaps in the evening before you fall asleep.

It's not going to help much if you take the attitude, "Okay. Rotella says I have to visualize, so I'm visualizing," any more than it would help you become a great sprinter if you jogged through your workouts. You must get emotionally charged. You must see things as if they're actually happening at the moment you are envisioning them. Feel the pinch as your wedge nips a pitch shot off a tight lie. Hear the thump as your club strikes the sand. You have to be immersed in it. Your mind will know if you're just going through the motions.

So, at this point you understand the mechanics of the short shots that trouble you and you've started to fix your mechanics if they need fixing. More important, you've begun working on changing your perception of yourself from someone with a yips problem to someone who knows how to hit the short-game shots, has a sound plan for improvement, and is executing that plan.

You need to check your pre-shot routine. I've talked about a sound routine, particularly its mental aspects. **Make sure you have a sound routine and begin to use it, even in practice.** You need to work on calming yourself down when you face a short-game shot, and your routine will help you do that. Work on having the same low level of intensity on every shot, whether it's around the practice green or out on the golf course.

And you will have to work. I don't know of an instant cure for a wrecked short game, but I've never failed to help a player who was committed to working on improvement. There's normally a progression to the way a player recovers his short game. At first he can hit one good shot out of five, even when he sets the ball up on a nice, plush lie. Then he moves to two or three out of five and then four out of five and finally five out of five. And as he does this, he's writing down his good shots, or taping them, or meditating on them, using his practice to help rebuild his confidence. He's changing the way he talks about his short game. When someone asks him how it's going, he says, "Getting better!" Or he says, "Great!"

Around this time, he rediscovers his touch. Once a player is making solid contact every time he pitches the ball or chips, he can start improving his command of trajectory and direction. He goes from hitting the ball somewhere near his target to hitting it to his target.

Now the improving player starts varying the lies he practices from. Instead of an easy, favorable lie, he puts the ball down in the rough and on thin, scraggly grass. He pitches from uphill lies, downhill lies, and sidehill lies. Then he starts playing games around the practice green with a buddy to get the taste of relying on his short game under pressure. After that, he should be able to take his short game out on the course when he's playing casual rounds. Then he does it playing for money against his friends. And finally, he's ready for a tournament. He's looking for opportunities to show off. When he misses a green, he thinks, *Now the fun starts!*

I have described this as a steady progression, but the likelihood is it won't be. There will be regression. You'll start to think you own it; you'll get cocky. And then you'll miss one. When you do, you're going to have to decide whether your response will be panic or acceptance. If you choose acceptance, you'll understand that no one is perfect and go back to the mental and physical fundamentals.

You might consider emulating the way a smart Tour player would react to a missed short-game shot. He wouldn't go back to the hotel with the memory of that missed shot still dominating his mind. He'd turn in his scorecard and go out to the short-game practice area and work until he'd supplanted the memory of that bad shot with the memory of dozens of good ones hit with the same club from a similar lie. Tour players never let their short games get into disarray because they catch a problem as it begins and fix it. You can do the same. Don't go home until you've fixed it.

If your problem is a wrecked putting stroke, and not wedge shots, you're a member of a dwindling tribe. In years past, I saw a lot of players who developed twitchy putting strokes. Almost always, this was a mental issue rather than a mechanical one. Players who said they had the yips were sometimes perfectionists who got obsessed with developing a perfect putting stroke. They were very conscious of the way their putter blade moved. Sometimes they were good enough with their long game that they realized their lack of success could only be attributed to putting; they put so much pressure on their putting that they cracked. In amateur circles, I tended to see people who were socially anxious and worried about what their friends would think if they missed short putts. All three types tended to berate themselves each time they missed a putt they thought they should have made. Their self-flagellation got worse if that putt happened to come at a crucial moment in a tournament or a match. Over time, they started to brood more and more about missed putts. And then, one day, they started to flinch as they brought the putter blade into contact with the ball on short putts.

I suspect that in some cases the so-called putting yips are a defensive mechanism employed by a battered psyche. If you're a perfectionist and you miss a three-foot putt, you have no one to blame but yourself—*unless you can blame a disease.* If the disease causes you to miss putts, then it's not your fault, any more than it's the fault of a man with arthritis that he can't go out and jog three miles. So if you get the yips, you don't have to beat yourself up.

Players like Harry Vardon, Sam Snead, and Ben Hogan saw the ends of their careers marred by the yips. They might not have suffered that embarrassment if they were playing today. Nowadays, when a player starts getting twitchy on the green, he has a variety of alternatives. There are long putters, belly putters, and putters that look like potato mashers. There are alternate grips—left hand low, claw, and so on. All of these are designed to give the player the feeling, at least, that his hands and wrists are immobilized, that they can't spasm the way they did when he used a conventional putter and grip.

As you know by now, I don't much care how a player moves his putter, or what putter he moves, as long as his mind is clear and he unconsciously focuses on a target and reacts to it. So if a player "cures" his putting ailment by going to one of these alternatives, I'm happy for him. I don't think the beneficial effect comes so much from the length of the putter as it does from the effect the new tool has on the player's mind and his confidence. But I see many players who have overcome bouts of the yips and extended their careers by changing putters and grips, and I am a big fan of whatever works.

If, however, you've tried those things, you still think you have the yips, and you've come to this book in search of a cure, you're going to have to grapple with the attitudes that brought the problem on.

Your first step is to abandon the conceit that you or anyone else ought to make all of his putts from within a certain range, whether it be two feet or six feet. No one does. Golfers miss short putts because they misread them, or because the green is lumpy, or for any number of other reasons, many of them having to do with where their minds are when they strike the ball. They miss them because they're human and humans are imperfect.

Acceptance, as you know, is part of a sound routine for all shots, including putts. Whatever happens with a putt means very little to a player who understands this. Three outcomes are possible when you hit a putt. It misses, and you putt again. It goes in the cup and you start thinking about your tee shot on the next hole. Or it falls in the cup and you add up the score and see how you did because there aren't any holes left to play. In none of those cases is there anything to be gained by anguishing over what happened to a putt. Remember to attach the same low level of importance to any shot, whether it's a practice putt before the round starts or a putt to win a match on the 18th green.

You need to consider your entire putting routine. Do you envision a troublesome putt going in, or do you worry that it's going to miss? As you stand over the ball and go through the final stages of your routine, does your mind remain clear? Or do you get conscious and start reminding yourself of ways to make your stroke do what you want it to do? Do you guide and steer the ball or let the stroke flow? Your goal must be a routine in which you make every putt in your mind, away from the ball; then, once you're over the ball, react indifferently to your target. Finally, you accept what happens.

One big step toward fixing your condition is a commitment that you will not hit a putt until your mind is where you want it to be. Another big step is deciding that you're more interested in your putting process than in your putting results. If you execute your routine, physically and mentally, a putt is a success regardless of whether it goes in. You can't control whether it goes in. You can only control the process.

Just as players who have issues with greenside wedge shots must work on their memories and self-image, so must a player with putting issues. The same tools—keeping a journal of successful shots, using video, and visualization—will help in this process. Milk each successful putt for all the self-confidence it can give you. Develop amnesia for putts that miss. Be your own cheerleader. When people ask you how you're playing, say, "I'm putting great!"

In one respect, fixing a wrecked putting game is easier than fixing wedge problems. You can (and should) go onto a practice green, although you can't practice your way out of the yips unless you make practice part of changing your mental approach. Try placing a few balls a short distance from a hole, so that you're bound to make nearly all of them. Start building memories of balls rolling into the hole. This is something you can't as easily do with pitches and chips and bunker shots. Take advantage of it.

Reinforce those memories by allowing yourself to feel some joy and satisfaction at seeing a ball roll into the hole. Your attitude should be *Another one falls! I'm good,* rather than *I'm only doing what any duffer could do.* Go through your routine on lots of practice putts, rehearsing the way you will envision success, and putt unconsciously. If you like, take a moment to imagine that you're putting not on the practice green, but on the 18th hole of a tournament you'd very much like to win. Feel the pressure. Feel the nerves. Make the putt. There's a lot of instinctive wisdom in the way youngsters play on a putting green, pretending they're TV announcers and murmuring, "He's got this four-footer for the U.S. Open championship."

As with chipping and pitching the ball, rebuilding a wrecked putting game is not an instant process. It's going to take a while. I can't say how long, because each case is different. A lot will depend on how you act on the realization that the so-called yips are a psychological problem, not a physical one, on how diligently you work on changing your attitude about putting.

Your goal is to become carefree and cocky. Start acting like you already are. Smile when you walk onto the green. This is the stage on which you're going to show off what you've accomplished with your putting. It's a party. Have fun at it.

Maybe you used to feel that way around the green but don't anymore. I can assure you that you can recapture that feeling and get more fun out of the game.

My friend Marty Jacobson did. I worked with Marty off and on when his short game went sour. But the more important work was what he did himself. He forged new memories, memories of successful shots. He worked on his mechanics. Gradually, his visualization got more powerful. He started to see himself hitting great chips and pitches again. At the same time, he no longer allowed his emotions to rule his reaction to the occasional bad wedge shot. Missing one meant very little to him. He renewed his belief that if he followed his routine, his results would usually be good.

I got a call from him a year or so ago in April. He was in Florida, where he'd been playing at a Society of Seniors event. I was at the Masters. Marty had been in a four-ball match with a good friend of his, Burke Hays; it went into sudden-death extra holes. On the fifth extra hole, a par three, Marty was off the green in a tight lie with his tee shot. He visualized his shot, went through his routine, and chipped up to three feet. Then he made his putt; his team won the match.

"Hey, I know you're at the Masters," Marty said on the phone. "But I've got more important things to talk about." He proceeded to tell me about his winning chip.

I laughed. I wouldn't have cared where he'd found me. I love getting calls like that.

TEN

PATIENCE AND PERSEVERANCE

The whole secret to mastering the game of golf—and this applies to the beginner as well as the pro—is to cultivate a mental approach to the game that will enable you to shrug off the bad shots, shrug off the bad days, keep patient, and know in your heart that sooner or later you will be back on top.

—Arnold Palmer

Clients and readers often ask a variation of the following question: "Doc, I believe what you've said about putting [or pitching, or chipping, or any other aspect of the game] and I'm trying to do those things. I'm doing my best to go unconscious. I'm practicing every day. But I don't see any difference in my scores. I don't see any difference in my short game on the course. Why haven't I gotten better? When will I?"

And I always reply, "I don't know."

Then I add, "But I know you will get better if you stick with it. It may take a month. It may take six months. It may take a year. But if you stick with it long enough, you'll see results. It's like riding a bicycle or lifting weights. You ride every day or lift every day. If you add minutes to every ride, eventually your endurance will improve. If you add weight to every workout, eventually your strength will improve. It gets easier. But it's not a race to see who gets there first. It's a competition to see who stays there the longest, so stick with it. It takes a lot of patience and perseverance, but there's no other way to lower your score."

Patience is golf's most underrated virtue and perhaps the hardest virtue to teach. I see a lot of players, amateurs and professionals alike, who can be patient as long as they're making huge steps forward. But as soon as the huge steps stop, so does their patience. To be successful, a golfer must learn to enjoy the challenge of improvement, to enjoy the journey. He must find pride in accepting the challenge. Rather than be frustrated by the journey's length, he must dwell on how good it will feel to finally arrive. Then, when he does arrive, he must accept a second challenge, the challenge of working hard to sustain his progress. He understands that this is why golf is never boring and why he loves it.

I'm talking about two variations of the same virtue. A player needs long-term patience as he pursues his goals. He needs short-term patience as he copes with the unexpected challenges a round of golf entails.

I know that every now and then, a researcher working in a lab somewhere will announce that he has discovered exactly how much long-term patience a player must have. The researcher will conclude some experiments and promulgate an ironclad rule: it takes ten thousand repetitions, or ten thousand hours of practice, or some other suspect number to learn a new technique and improve. I have yet to see evidence that such a "rule" is very useful in predicting how long it will take a golfer to improve. Too much depends on the player and his attitude. Too much depends on the way a player practices and the skill of his teacher.

A good teacher can definitely accelerate the process in several ways. The good teacher believes in the pupil and encourages the pupil. This adds to the pupil's motivation and confidence. A good teacher devises improvement strategies that are tailored to the player's learning style. He provides drills that help the player incorporate new moves more quickly. He teaches practice strategies that pay off in faster progress. He provides accurate and useful feedback about what a player is doing right and what he still needs to change.

I believe that's why Bob Jones and Tiger Woods, who had excellent instruction as boys, were able to dominate world golf in their twenties, while Ben Hogan, who was largely self-taught, didn't win anything until he was in his thirties and forties. The lesson here is that Hogan was smart enough to believe in himself and to persevere. Eventually, he got there. Were it not for his patience, he wouldn't have.

Too many players who don't practice nearly as much as Hogan did don't understand the importance of his patience. They use the practice they do put into their games as a rationalization for anger and irritation. Maybe they don't see improvement, so they get frustrated and angry. Maybe they see improvement in the practice area, but they can't take it to the course. They get angry. Sometimes they give up.

Don't use your practice and your hard work as a pretext for being angry and impatient. Don't have the mentality, "I've worked so hard.

I deserve to be rewarded." When a player tells me that, my response is, "Oh, so you made a deal with the devil that if you practice a certain amount, he's going to make you win?" It doesn't work that way.

You can increase the chances that you'll play better if you practice and work on your short game. And I have never seen a case where a player practiced intelligently and persistently and didn't improve eventually. But there are no guarantees in golf. There's certainly no guarantee on how fast improvement will happen.

But the player who practices diligently and struggles to be patient is acting more rationally than the player who can't or won't practice and still gets impatient.

Some amateurs have a million things going on in their lives—jobs, families, kids, and responsibilities. They can only get away to play golf once in a while, and they can't prepare or practice in between rounds. If that describes you, you need above all to be honest with yourself about where your game is. You need to pick your targets with the 80 percent rule in mind. You need to work doubly hard to clear your mind before every shot, particularly short game shots. You need to make your best effort to hit them unconsciously. Most of all, you need to be certain that acceptance is part of your routine. Acceptance is essential to acquiring patience.

Yet I see players who rarely, if ever, practice nevertheless get impatient and angry. I see players who clutter their minds with mechanical thoughts get impatient and upset when their shots are awkward and unsuccessful. They would be doing themselves a favor if they learned to smile when they mishit a shot, shrug their shoulders, and accept the fact that being a spouse, a breadwinner, and a parent may not be compatible with immediately playing the golf of their dreams.

The best example I know of to illustrate the kind of long-term patience I am talking about is my friend Gary Burkhead. Gary spent the better part of his life in the financial business, where he did very well. He played golf occasionally and had a handicap in the teens. That was understandable. He worked twelve to fourteen hours a day.

He retired at sixty and decided that he would like to become a scratch player and play in the U.S. Senior Amateur. Considering where he was starting, that was a very lofty goal. Gary goes about reaching it in a very systematic way. He rises early and works out with a trainer. He practices and plays golf from five to ten hours a day, concentrating particularly on his short game. He takes lessons, including short-game lessons. He is a dedicated individual.

But what I most admire about Gary is his patience and persistence. He's had some setbacks in his quest, which is now ten years long. He's still looking to qualify for the U.S. Senior Amateur. But he has never wavered in his commitment. His ball-striking has gotten solid and consistent. He's gotten very good at his short shots. His handicap nowadays is in the very low single digits. I don't know for sure that he'll make the field for the Senior Amateur, but I wish that every player I work with had his patience and persistence. Most amateurs would not have stayed with an improvement plan the way Gary has. They would not have enjoyed the success he has enjoyed.

Gary's patience has already rewarded him. Whether or not he achieves all his goals, he will have the satisfaction of knowing that he gave them his best. He will know what his potential was. He will have pride in the cool, calm, and unflappable way he has pursued his golfing dreams. Not many amateurs can say that, because very few have the requisite patience and persistence.

It's a bit easier for me to understand impatience on the part of professionals. Unlike most amateurs, they *have* put in the practice time. Their livelihoods and their professional reputations are at stake. They've committed their lives to being as good as they can possibly be. When it doesn't happen, they can get frustrated and impatient. On the Tour, when you're playing well, you're Joe Stud. Everyone fawns over you. When you're not playing well, it can seem that no one has time for you. Agents and sponsors start to nitpick. Galleries leave you and the media no longer want your opinion. It's easy to panic.

But I have rarely seen frustration or impatience work as positive forces for a professional golfer. In a few cases, if impatience spurs a player who has been coasting to do the work he ought to do, it might be helpful. Far more often, though, I've seen impatience undermine a player's game. In the middle of a round, he might get impatient and turn on his conscious brain, trying to force his body to produce a certain shot. Instead, he hits it sideways. Or he starts making unwise decisions, trying to force birdies to happen rather than following a wise game plan, using good course management, and waiting for the birdies to come. **One of the best adages a golfer can follow is to always play with a conservative strategy and a cocky swing. That is, pick a shot you're fully confident you can hit, then swing confidently. If a player picks a shot he isn't confident about, his swing will reflect that doubt. Impatience leads to that mistake.**

Impatience can damage a pro after his round is over. A Tour player whose impatience tips him over into panic mode finds a thousand teachers. Everyone has a tip for him and he listens to all of them. He bounces from teacher to teacher, from method to method. He can't seem to arrive at a set of fundamentals he believes in and get them ingrained so he can play with a quiet mind. When a teacher does offer him some sensible advice, he often perceives the teacher's suggested path as taking too long. He's looking for an instant solution, one that usually doesn't exist. Soon, he's lost.

Sometimes, golf's demand for patience is more subtle. If a golfer wins the United States Amateur Championship, he of course receives no money. But he does get invitations to three of the following year's major championships: the Masters and the United States and British Opens. When Peter Uihlein won the Amateur on his twenty-first birthday in 2010, those invitations were among the first things he thought of. He correctly anticipated the thrill of playing in those events. He did not anticipate, at least not completely, the patience they would require.

Peter swung his first golf club (a plastic one) before he learned to walk. He's been the top-ranked American junior golfer and the top-ranked amateur in the world. He has set his sights on becoming the world's best golfer, period. He wanted very much to do well in those three majors. He took his first opportunity to play at Augusta in October 2010, six months before the tournament.

Peter had a good attitude toward the majors. He told himself that he'd won the Amateur at Chambers Bay, a long, difficult course set up by the USGA. He reminded himself that the course he played for his college team, Karsten Creek at Oklahoma State, was extremely demanding. He told himself he needn't worry that the golf courses he would play in his majors would be too tough for him. He told himself that whether it was called a major championship or not, he would still just be playing golf with his own clubs and balls. He prepared to underreact to everything. He told himself to enjoy the experience and the challenge.

All of these were good ideas and they stood Peter in good stead. But he still found that he needed to work on his patience.

Peter got off to a great start at the Masters, making birdies on the second and third holes. He was even par beginning the second nine. But he hit his approach over the green on No. 10, and he couldn't get up and down. That's when he started feeling impatient. "I got frustrated with myself, and I wouldn't just let it go and play," he said. He was five over par after two rounds and missed the cut.

Peter realized his frustration hadn't helped him, but realizing that fact and acting on it are tough lessons for a young golfer. Every amateur in a major championship has a couple of secondary goals. He wants to make the cut and he wants to be low amateur. At the U.S. Open at Congressional, Peter wanted those things for himself.

But each day his round got off to a slow start. He double-bogeyed the first hole on Thursday. He bogeyed No. 10, the first hole he played, on Friday. "It seemed like each day I got behind the eight ball early and tried to fight back by forcing the issue," he said later. As he played his second nine on Friday, he was aware that the cut was likely to be four over par, and he was seven over. He birdied the 5th hole and came to the par-five 6th. He was two shots over the projected cut line, thinking he had to seize the chance to make a birdie. His mind was attuned too much to results and that ended up costing him.

Peter hit two fine shots on No. 6, but he caught a bad break. Feeling that he needed a birdie, he had gone for the green with his second shot. His ball cleared the water hazard in front of the green but plugged in a greenside bunker. He hit a good explosion shot. I was watching, and I thought it would leave him with at least a birdie putt. But the ball landed on what must have been the hardest surface at Congressional, took off, and rolled into the water. Peter played well to finish the hole with a bogey. But he had lost his patience. Not coincidentally, he bogeyed two of his remaining holes. He missed the cut again.

This is the way young players learn. At the British Open, Peter applied the lessons from Augusta and Congressional. Again, he got off to a rocky start, with bogeys on two of his first three holes. But he steadied himself, didn't press, and plugged away. He made a few birdies on the back nine for a 71. He repeated that the next day and made the cut. He went on to finish tied for 48th, beating a number of established pros, including the defending champion, Louis Oosthuizen. It was a great accomplishment.

"I learned that you don't have to be perfect to make the cut and contend on the highest level," Peter told me later. "I got a bad wind on Saturday morning, and I found out that you can hit good shots and get a bad break, and vice versa."

He was able to maintain his composure better, to stay in the present better, and thus to score better. "You can't let those things affect you," Peter said, referring to errant shots and errant bounces. "The number one lesson was patience." He honored his commitment to stay with the process and avoid thinking about results. He competed with himself, not against other players. He took a huge step in the process of putting his ultimate golf game together.

If Peter can remember that, and continue to practice it, I have no doubt that he'll qualify for many majors as a pro. And he could win some, if he continues to honor his commitment to patience, regardless of all the things that will happen to him on the golf course.

But that's a demanding challenge for a good young pro, because the nature of the good young pro is that he's rarely satisfied by his accomplishments, at least not for very long. That's a good thing, because it means that he's always got an incentive to work hard and improve. But if dissatisfaction spills over into impatience, it can be damaging.

I was reminded of this when I started working with Keegan Bradley halfway through his first year on the Nationwide Tour. I'd heard a lot about Keegan over the years from his aunt Pat. She'd told me how talented he was and what a good kid he was. And everything Pat had said turned out to be true when I met Keegan.

I took him out to Farmington Country Club in Charlottesville and we played a round with a couple of friends of mine, Jimmy Cassella and Don Robertson. Keegan at this time was hardly a household name. He'd played his junior golf in New England. He'd played college golf at St. John's in New York City. And though he'd done well, neither Massachusetts high school championships nor success in the Big East attract much attention. Keegan had gone on to the Hooters Tour for a couple of years, paying his dues. He'd worked his way up to the Nationwide Tour. But when we met, he'd missed a few cuts and hadn't won much money. (He went on to finish 14th on the Nationwide money list in 2010 and qualify for the 2011 PGA Tour.)

Keegan shot 63 that day at Farmington, equaling the course record. Jimmy Cassella was impressed. "Keegan, we have a tournament here every year called the Kenridge Invitational. You could win it," he said. I laughed. The Kenridge is a fine tournament, but it's for amateurs. The talent I had seen on the Farmington course that morning was capable of winning much more than that. In fact, I've since enjoyed calling Jimmy when Keegan wins on the PGA Tour and saying, "You know, Jimmy, you might be right. Maybe Keegan could win the Kenridge."

Keegan reminded me of his aunt Pat in some ways. There's a family resemblance around the eyes. Keegan shares Pat's work ethic. But Pat was very intense, very driven. When she was competing, especially early in her career, her life consisted of practicing, playing, and practicing some more. Keegan is more fun-loving.

But, like Pat, he is very teachable. If Keegan asks for advice and he likes what he hears, he adopts the suggestion wholeheartedly, whether it comes from me or his swing coach, Jim McLean. Before the Byron Nelson this year, he called me and told me he was worried about the tee shot on the closing hole, a dogleg par four. The drive had to be threaded down a wind-whipped fairway that sloped toward a water hazard on the left and was guarded by trees on the right.

I told Keegan that I didn't care what club he used for that shot, but I thought he needed to be absolutely certain he hit it without fear, decisively and unconsciously. If he could do that, I said, he'd have an advantage over the rest of the field. Keegan did that during the tournament. He parred the 18th each day during the weekend, including in the playoff, which he won from Ryan Palmer.

Keegan, like a typical rookie, had fairly modest goals for his first couple of events on the Tour. He wanted to make the cuts. And he did make the cut in his first event, the Sony Open in Hawaii. He birdied the final hole to get under the line by a stroke. But because the event was shortened by rain, not everyone who made the cut and made a check got to play the final two rounds. When Keegan called me, he was disappointed that he hadn't played the final two rounds, disappointed that he hadn't played better. I liked hearing that, but I also needed to remind him about being patient.

"I want you to focus on the birdie you made on the last hole to get under the cut line," I said. "Focus on the fact that you made a nice check that paid for your expenses out there. This tour is going to beat you up and keep giving you reasons to get down on yourself, to be impatient. You've got to keep finding the good in your play, keep finding reasons to be optimistic and patient."

Keegan worked on that, just as he worked on all the facets of his game. But it wasn't easy. After he won the Byron Nelson, the temptation of impatience grew stronger rather than weaker. He started thinking about the majors he would like to play in and the invitational events he'd get into if he cracked the top 50 in the world rankings. He started thinking about the Presidents Cup and Ryder Cup teams.

When I talked to him prior to the PGA Championship in Atlanta, he was still disappointed by the way he'd played at the Bridgestone Invitational at Firestone the week before. Keegan had opened with a 67 and a 65 to tie for the lead. He had a 68 in the third round and slipped two shots off the pace. In the final round, he made four bogeys and a double on the final nine holes to shoot 74 and fall into a tie for 15th place.

"I had a chance to win and I really got in my way," he said. "I got ahead of myself. I started thinking about being in the top fifty, getting into the Masters and the U.S. Open and the British Open, and I put a lot of pressure on myself." He told me he felt he hadn't lived up to the Bradley standard set by Aunt Pat. "I've got to do a better job of being into the process, not the results," he said.

I liked hearing that. It meant that Keegan had learned the main lesson from his experience in Akron. It meant that Keegan wanted to address his mistakes honestly and wasn't afraid to talk about them. **On the golf course, a player with a good mental game concentrates on what he can control and only on what he can control. He can control his own adherence to his routine, making sure that he does everything he can to make each shot a success. Thoughts about what might happen in the future only clutter the mind.**

When a kid is doing as well as Keegan was, a big part of my job is just pointing that out to him, making sure his perception is realistic. There was much to be happy about in the way Keegan had played.

"I started working with your aunt Pat when she was thirty-one. You're twenty-five and you're way ahead of where she was at that age," I told Keegan. "I love the fact that you're getting in position to win and you've already won once. You can't let having a great tournament and not getting all of it turn into a negative. You've got to look at yourself as you look at the Red Sox and the Celtics—you're an undying fan. When they don't manage to pull one out, you look for the bright spots and feel confident about the next game. Be the same way about yourself."

Keegan told me he felt more pressure because his mother, sister, and nephew were in Atlanta to watch him. He didn't want to disappoint them.

"No matter what you do, you're going to be a star to them and they'll still love you and be proud of you," I said. "Don't pretend that they won't. Besides, your nephew is a year old. I promise you he doesn't know anything about golf. He just wants to play with his uncle. So use that to take your mind off golf."

We talked a lot about underresponding and underreacting to anything that might happen during the tournament. **Emotional responses and overreactions are the enemies of patience. If you're calm, even phlegmatic, you're more likely to be patient. I like players to enjoy their good shots, within reason. That helps reinforce confidence-building memories. But I like them to shrug at bad shots and move on.**

Keegan took that in. But, of course, there were tests of patience still to come. The greatest of them came during the final round on the 15th hole, a brutal, 250-yard par three guarded by water that he triple-bogeyed. Keegan told me later he thought he'd hit a great tee shot, but the ball bounced into some of the nastiest rough on the course, just behind the green. He did a good job of underreacting to that unfortunate bounce. And, he told me later, he did a good job of just seeing and hitting his chip shot onto the green. But, as is often the case in major championships, the green was as crusty as month-old bread.

When the ball went in the water, Keegan could have folded, and I'm sure that a lot of the viewers figured that the tournament belonged to Jason Dufner. Keegan was able to clear his mind and hit a good wedge to the green from the drop zone. And then he had another test of patience. His putt for double-bogey just missed. Keegan thought he'd made it, but it broke a little more than he'd anticipated.

For four or five seconds, Keegan's mind wandered. He thought he'd blown the tournament. He would have had to be superhuman *not* to have such thoughts at least cross his mind. But the test of a good golfer is not whether he bars all distracting or negative thoughts from his mind during a competitive round. If that were the test, nearly every golfer would fail. The test is whether the golfer regains control of his mind once that distracting thought creeps in.

I should point out here that Keegan had some help in passing this test, and it came from his pairing partner, Scott Verplank. When Keegan missed his putt for double bogey, he took a few steps without thinking of where he was. Almost immediately, he caught himself and worried that he'd stepped in the line of Scott's next putt—a breach of etiquette, especially considering that Scott was still in the running.

Upset, Keegan walked carefully to Scott and said, "Scott, I am so sorry if I stepped in your line."

Scott could have said something curt or something nasty. He could have scowled and said nothing. Had he done so, it would have been that much harder for Keegan to recover his poise. Instead, he gave Keegan a quick grin and said, "Nah, I'm great." When Keegan told me about this, he was still impressed by Scott's sportsmanship. So was I.

Keegan was able to get back to his golf game. The first order of business was making the putt for his triple-bogey six on No. 15. The next was clearing his mind for the tee shot on the 16th. He told me later on that he had felt like he had me sitting on his shoulder at times during that PGA, something his aunt Pat had said during her career, too.

"You had told me if I ever started thinking about results and stuff like that to just break out grinning and say, 'You silly son of a gun. Come on. It's okay. Now, let's just go play the next shot.' And I just started immediately getting back into thinking about hitting a great drive on the next hole. And, Doc, I may have hit the best drive I hit all week on that tee shot," Keegan said.

Keegan's play over the next three holes is the best illustration I can give you of how patience, perseverance, and commitment to the process of playing great golf work.

His long, accurate tee shot on 16 led to a birdie, which he followed by draining a long putt on 17 for another birdie. He and his caddie, Steve "Pepsi" Hale, approached the 18th. With the possible exception of the closing hole at Carnoustie, the 18th at the Atlanta Athletic Club may be the most challenging final hole I've seen on a major championship golf course. It's 490 yards long, and the tee shot must be placed between a lake and a series of deep bunkers. Since the hole is so long, the tee shot has to be long as well as precise. The second shot has to carry the water to reach the green.

Keegan asked Pepsi what club he ought to hit. I love the way Pepsi replied. "You're going to rip a 2-iron like you've been doing all week," he said. Pepsi earned a spot in the ranks of great caddies with that response. He reminded Keegan to stick with his game plan. He reminded him of the successful shots he'd hit on that hole earlier. He reminded him to swing confidently. Keegan did. He very nearly birdied the 18th. His par put him in a three-hole playoff.

In the playoff, Keegan birdied No. 16 again to give himself the ostensible winning margin. But I remain convinced that Keegan's real winning margin was the patience and perseverance he summoned in the face of adversity. Not many people remember it, but he had double-bogeyed the first hole on Saturday during the PGA. A lot of young players would have lost their patience then, especially coming off a tough week like the one Keegan had in Akron. Others would have fallen apart after the triple bogey at No. 15 on Sunday. But Keegan stayed patient and persevered.

As he told me later, "I learned that you don't have to be perfect if you let nothing bother you and underreact to everything."

ELEVEN

STAYING IN THE MOMENT

It is useless to attempt to guess what someone else may do,
and worse than useless to set a score for yourself to play for.
—Bobby Jones

Keegan Bradley won the PGA Championship because, showing unusual patience, maturity, and wisdom for a twenty five-year-old in that situation, he managed to use one of the most valuable mental skills in golf. He stayed in the moment.

When I say he "stayed in the moment," I mean that he didn't think about the past, which included the bad hop and the unfortunate chip that had befallen him on the 15th hole. He didn't think about the future, which included whatever the outcome of the tournament would be, and what people would think of him, and the things he might think about himself. He got control of his mind and he focused on the only important thing, his next shot. It happened to be the tee shot on the 16th hole, and he hammered it. Keegan stayed in the moment for each of the ensuing 18 shots of that tournament, including the playoff. He played them each in turn, giving each his full attention.

To my way of thinking, it wouldn't have mattered much if Jason Dufner had held on to the lead he had over Keegan when he started the 15th hole. Keegan would still have been a winner because he had controlled everything he could control. That's the nature of golf. Sometimes you do everything you want to do, you stay in the moment for every shot, and someone else posts a score a stroke or two lower than your own. There's nothing you can do about it except take your hat off, smile, and shake his hand. On that particular day, he was *the* winner. But you're *a* winner if you stay in the moment on every shot, controlling every aspect of the game that you can control.

I remember Padraig Harrington coming to talk one Friday evening at Augusta when he'd just missed the cut at the Masters. Some players would have wanted to vent about what went wrong. Not Padraig. He'd had some bad bounces and some putts that lipped out. But what he took away from that tournament was this:

"I know now that I can win majors," he told me. "I know I can handle my mind and emotions. I had my head where I wanted it to be on every shot today. I know now I can do it."

"Beautiful," I said.

Not long thereafter, Padraig proved himself a prophet by winning not one but three majors, two British Opens and a PGA. He laid the groundwork for those triumphs when he missed the cut at the Masters but understood that he was a winner because he'd controlled his mind and emotions and stayed in the moment for every shot.

I think about this element of the game when I hear a discussion of whether professional golfers should or should not look at leaderboards as they play, especially during the final few holes of a tournament. Sometimes a macho element gets tossed into the discussion, as in, "What are you, afraid to look at leaderboards?"

There may not be leaderboards around the course when the average golfer plays, but same issue arises in a slightly different guise. Should a player keep track of his score during a round? Should he play differently if he's down or up in a match?

My answer comes down to how an individual defines greatness in golf, or in any other sport. I think the great players are those who get lost in their own little world, playing their own games and controlling their minds and emotions, staying in the moment. At the highest level, this sort of player is going to win major championships. But at other levels, she's going to win club championships. She's going to be a great partner in a member-guest. She'll break 100 for the first time and be thrilled about it. To me, greatness has many levels.

That's why I recommend to professional players that they not look at leaderboards during a tournament. It's why I recommend to club golfers that they play every shot as if it were a shot in a stroke-play competition. I don't care if the format is actually match play or if they're two up or three down. This is the way they're going to stay in the moment and achieve greatness. By definition, staying in the moment precludes thinking about anything other than your own next shot. Staying in the moment maximizes the chance that you'll hit that shot successfully. So why would you let a leaderboard, which is about what others are doing, or the status of a match, take you out of that little world?

You must be secure enough to believe that if you play your

best you will be a winner. You must understand that winning the battle with yourself is all you can do.

This principle applies to many sports. My friend John Calipari had a young and inexperienced basketball team at Kentucky during the most recent college basketball season. The team got off to a slow start. Cal decided to tell his players to stop looking at the scoreboard, stop caring about winning or losing, and to think only about executing the offense and defense he'd taught them. "I'll look at the scoreboard," he said, "and if we need to make adjustments or changes, I'll make them. You guys just go play basketball."

After he told them that, Cal's team didn't lose a game until it had reached the Final Four and ran into the ultimate champion, Connecticut.

Great football coaches, like Nick Saban at Alabama, also emphasize the process. They tell their players that if they keep their attention on the process, giving their utmost every step of the way, the results will take care of themselves.

You'll recall from the first chapter that Trevor Immelman tries to avoid looking at leaderboards when he's playing. "When I turned pro," Trevor says, "I felt I was watching the leaderboards too much and changing my strategy based on what I saw. I'd get too defensive or too aggressive. So I decided not to look. I feel it takes more discipline and confidence not to look at them. You have to believe that your best golf will be good enough to win if you can just play it."

You'll recall that Trevor had established a game plan for Augusta National that he felt gave him his best chance to shoot a low score. You should have such a plan for every competitive round you play. It should include a governing principle like the 80 percent rule that will determine how you pick targets and select strategies for the short-game shots that arise during a round.

So if you have such a plan, and you know it's designed to help you shoot your best possible score, why would you give the plan up because of something you see on a leaderboard or because you're two down with four to play? What possible situation would cause you to want to play less than your best golf?

When I discuss this issue with players, they invariably ask something like this: "But suppose the last hole is a par five with a pond in front of the green, and I'm one shot behind. Don't I want to know that before I make up my mind whether to go for the green with my second shot? Don't I want to kick it up another gear?"

I reply that if a player needs a birdie on a par-five final hole, there are lots of ways to make it. Going for the green with a heroic, high-risk second shot that he wouldn't try on Thursday is not the most promising strategy to give the player what he wants. He's more likely to make it by ignoring the leaderboard, following his game plan, laying up to a favorite distance, hitting a wedge close, and making the putt. That's why the short game is so important. That's why great players work so hard at it. Yet I've seen many players look at leaderboards, forget about their game plans, and hit disastrous shots due to spur-of-the-moment, emotional thinking.

The virtues of staying in the moment apply doubly to the short game. If you've got a good plan and a good mental game, you're already going to be putting to make all your putts. You're going to be trying to sink most, if not all, of your pitches and bunker shots. Why would knowing about the score, or thinking about the match situation, help you do these things any better?

Furthermore, the notion that the tournament or match situation should change the way you play usually assumes that you can predict how your opponent will play. You may arrive at the 16th tee two down. You may be tempted to think you have to find a way to force a couple of birdies to have a chance. But in my experience, that's often giving too much credit to the opposition. I've seen more matches and more tournaments won by someone who continues to play his own game in the last few holes while his opponent gets distracted and makes a couple of bogeys.

I know the lore of the game is full of tales that suggest the opposite. In these stories, the hero always checks the leaderboard, hitches up his pants, looks once into the adoring eyes of his girlfriend or his mother for inspiration, then hits a miraculous shot that hangs forever in the air, barely clears the hazard, and sends the crowd into paroxysms of ecstasy.

There are also stories of players who find "an extra gear" in certain situations. Davis Love once recounted to me how he'd played with Ben Crenshaw just before the 1994 Masters. Ben was off his game—hitting it all over the place. Then Ben's beloved teacher, Harvey Penick, died. Ben went to the funeral, flew back to Augusta, and won the Masters. He was the last guy Davis expected to win, based on his previous form. But Ben's grief over his teacher's death somehow helped him play his best. It helped him find an extra gear. But that doesn't invalidate the principle that staying in the moment is the best strategy for nearly all players.

I think there are a few athletes, like Ben Crenshaw in golf or John McEnroe in tennis, who were childhood prodigies, so talented that they have a tendency to get a little disinterested sometimes. McEnroe often played mediocre tennis in the early rounds of a tournament, going extra sets against lesser players, arguing with officials. Then in the finals, he seemed to find an "extra gear." This kind of prodigy might need some kind of mental kick in the pants—like being in the final—to force him finally to concentrate, go unconscious, and produce his best effort. But most of us don't need that sort of spur. The mere fact of playing in a tournament is more than enough to hold our attention. A look at the leaderboard isn't necessary.

Amateur golfers, when they play a regular Saturday-morning four-ball with their friends, like to have a small bet riding on the outcome. The competition and the bet make the match a little more interesting and challenging. They're a way to make sure the match gets their attention.

But good club players, in my experience, don't go from paying attention to being obsessed with where the match stands and who's pressing whom. They may be aware of it, if only because the other players in the foursome are talking about it. But they try not to let the match situation mean anything to them. Their goal is still to give every shot the same level of importance and to execute their game plan. They're still trying calmly to putt or pitch or chip the ball in the hole, regardless of whether they're up or down at the time.

There's a lesson to be learned from casual match play about the most effective attitude for a golfer. I see a lot of club players who are at their best in a four-ball match where they're getting strokes off the opposition. I'm not talking about sandbaggers here, about people who stretch the rules to get themselves fallaciously high handicaps. I'm talking about players who have the appropriate handicap. They play better in the four-ball matches where they're getting strokes because the circumstances relax them. They feel that they don't have to be perfect, either because their partners will pick them up if they have a bad hole or because they can afford a mediocre shot if they're getting a handicap stroke. They play much worse if they're in a stroke-play event where they're going to see a gross score go up next to their name at the end of the day.

The point is that most players are at their best when they're interested and engaged yet calm and relaxed and not worried about making a mistake. So why would the average player want to ratchet up the pressure he feels by looking at a leaderboard or paying close attention to the match score?

There is no rule about this, and I can't tell you that you'll never do well if you make yourself aware of the situation as you play. If you're a professional who's won a lot recently, and you look at the leaderboard and see that you have a one-stroke lead with four holes to play, there isn't likely to be much impact on your emotions. Your reaction is likely to be, *Okay. I've been here before and I know how to do this.* You'll stay in the moment.

But if you haven't won a lot, and won recently, or if you're an amateur who's never won the club championship or hasn't won it recently, what will your response be? Will you stay in the moment, or will you be distracted by thoughts of winning or losing?

I can't answer that question for you. But I do know what I would do.

TWELVE

PRACTICING YOUR SHOTS

It's not just about having the best players. It's about being relentless in the pursuit of your goal and resilient in the face of bad luck and adversity.

—Nick Saban

I'm putting my thoughts about practicing the short game toward the end of this book, but it's not because I don't think short-game practice is important. On the contrary. All of the good professional players I know spend hours practicing virtually every day, and the smartest among them devote the bulk of that time to practicing the short game.

I've waited until now because I know that not everyone can devote that kind of time to golf. I know that many golfers are hard-pressed just to get out to the course for a round once a week. Commitments to jobs and families prevent them from practicing. Or they live in cities and can't get to a course to practice. Such is modern life.

If you can't practice at all, you need to accept the fact that your golf will reflect this. Golf swings require complex skills, and those skills quickly atrophy if they're not practiced and maintained. Maintenance is one reason that professionals, who already know how to hit the shots, spend so much time in the practice area. You didn't have their skills to begin with, and you haven't maintained what you did have. So it's going to pay you not to be a perfectionist when you do go out to play. **There's nothing less rational than a player who never practices losing his temper when he hits a bad shot. If you never practice, don't try too hard or care too much.**

Instead, make up your mind that you're at least going to have a sound, simple routine on every shot. If, for example, you're hitting a pitch shot, be certain that your routine includes seeing the shot you want. Then feel the shot you want—take a practice swing or two, if that helps you. Then let it go, without worrying about hitting a bad shot, about chunking it or skulling it. Accept what happens, find the ball, and do it again. This routine is something you can rehearse mentally in the car as you drive to the course.

I think too many golfers assume that if they can't get out to a course, or at least to a driving range, they can't practice. **The truth is that a lot of valuable practice can take place indoors, at night.** If you can take fifteen minutes or half an hour in the evening, after the kids have gone to bed, you can help your short game. You don't even need to have a ball. In fact, a ball may be detrimental to this sort of practice.

Take putting, for instance. You can lay a mirror on the floor. Take a grease pencil or a marker and make a dot on the mirror. That dot will represent the middle of the ball. Grip your putter and take your putting stance as if there were a ball where the dot is. Check the position of your eyes in relation to the dot. They should be directly over it or perhaps a shade to the inside. If they're not, move until they are. Practice taking your putting stance until you can do it unconsciously, with your eyes always in the right position over the ball.

You've now honed one of the most important physical parts of a good putting routine.

Indoor practice without a ball is a good place to work on your putting stroke, too. This is the only place I like to see players working with one of the practice aids that aim to help a player feel a "correct" putting stroke. I don't like to see players using them on an actual green, with a ball and a hole. On a green, players should be focused on their target, not the arc of their stroke. If they want to work on the arc of their strokes, I tell players to do it at night, without a ball. Then it's fine.

A mirror, this time on a wall, can be helpful in practicing pitching and chipping, too. As I've mentioned, it's important to leave the conscious brain out of your pre-shot routine as much as possible. At the same time, players want to be precise about the way they set up for a shot—their grip, stance, posture. Using tape, mark the mirror at the points where you should see your shoulders, knees, and eyes when you line up for a shot. Practice getting into that position. Be as conscious as you like indoors until you can do the move instinctively. Go unconscious when you get outside.

If you're fortunate enough to have some time to practice your short game outdoors, how should you spend that time? There isn't a single answer that applies to everyone. Your practice needs depend on the state of your game.

If you're a beginner, or you're rebuilding a seriously flawed aspect of your game, you might need to spend more time on what Bob Christina calls "skills practice." We can also call it hitting balls in the training mode.

In skills practice, or the training mode, you're trying to develop those neural networks that govern a correct movement. Your conscious brain will be part of this process. Let's suppose you're trying to learn a basic pitch shot or improve one that has regressed. At this stage in your development, you may need to work with a bucket of balls and hit the same shot over and over again.

As I've said, I don't believe there is a magic number of times you have to repeat a motion until you've learned it. It varies with the individual and how he practices. A good teacher can watch you practice and give you feedback that can shorten the process. You never want to be practicing the wrong moves.

Bob Christina and others, notably Gabriele Wulf, have done research that suggests your learning will be faster if you and your teacher can come up with "external cues." An internal cue is a directive from your mind to your body to perform a certain motion. Your focus is on swing mechanics and how to move. You may, for example, tell your body to strike the ball on the downswing as you practice pitching, clipping the ball before the sole of the club hits the turf. With an external cue, something outside of your mind is added to the operation. The focus of your attention shifts from the movement to the way the movement affects something in the environment. Bob, for instance, likes to put a towel on the ground behind the ball when a student is learning a pitch shot. The towel encourages the student to focus on moving the club head (an external cue) so that it misses the towel (the second external cue) on the downswing. If the student doesn't do it correctly, the club head will hit the towel and the ball won't go anywhere.

Bob likes to have students use external cues in a three-step practice process. If you were using Bob's towel cue, for example, the first step would be to practice the swing with the towel but without a ball. You could practice in slow motion if you like. In step two, you'd put a ball down and hit it, using the towel to reinforce the idea of hitting on the downswing with the proper angle of approach. And in step three, you'd take away the towel or move to the side and hit the ball once or twice, trying to imagine the towel as you swung. Then you'd repeat the process until you could hit your chip or pitch shots consistently and proficiently.

Many of the drills that golf pros have long prescribed for their pupils use the principle of external cues. They accelerate the learning process. There is almost no end to them. You might, for example, draw parallel lines in front of and behind your ball in the practice bunker. Try to remove the sand between those lines. You can stretch a piece of string a foot off the ground, perpendicular to the line of a chip shot. Try to chip the ball under the string; this helps a student learn to hit down on the ball. I'm not suggesting that these external-cue drills are right for you. They are just a few examples.

Your teacher should be the person who prescribes drills and external cues for you. Remember that their purpose is to make it possible to move more quickly into practicing in the trusting mode. In the trusting mode, you think the way you intend to think on the course. You react to the target without conscious thought. Before you're ready for tournament golf, you need to be spending all, or nearly all, of your practice time in the trusting mode.

Almost as important as getting to the trusting mode is practicing in a way that transfers most effectively to the physical and mental environment you will find on the golf course. I'll talk about these one at a time.

The physical environment of the golf course bears little resemblance to the typical driving range. Even if your range has grass tees, all the shots you hit on it will come from roughly the same flat lie. Since the typical range has a wide open landing area, you're not going to simulate the act of hitting to a precise target by simply standing on the practice tee and hitting balls. And you'll almost never hit a pitch shot or a chip from a flat, uniform lie like you'll find on a practice tee.

So, it's important to find a way to simulate golf-course conditions when you practice. It goes without saying that you ought to use the targets your range provides and try to hit them rather than just hitting into space. Beyond that, you need to chip and pitch balls and hit bunker shots from all kinds of lies and all kinds of stances to all kinds of targets. You need to hit over hazards.

Fortunately, many newer clubs have realized this and designed short-game practice areas that incorporate these options. If you have access to such a facility, use it. When you practice there, make sure to give yourself sidehill lies, downhill lies, and uphill lies. Practice when the ground is wet. Practice from the rough. Practice off bare dirt and hardpan. Practice off thin lies. Practice pitching the ball over bunkers and stopping it with backspin. Practice pitches that roll out to an uphill target. As you improve, don't hit to the same target twice.

But even if you do all this, you're likely to find that your best practice will be out on the golf course. This is not something that a lot of golf-course superintendents will want to read. And I sympathize with them. They have a tough job, and it becomes impossible if golfers abuse the course when they practice. So if you practice on the course, be a good citizen about it. Don't take two shots from the same area. Carefully fill in or replace any divots you take. Rake the bunkers behind you.

That said, I like to see players going out to play a few holes in the twilight, or at some other time when the course is lightly used, with two or three extra balls in their pockets. Play one ball from the tee to the green. But when you get near the green, drop the other balls in places that have given you trouble in the past. Maybe one will go at the bottom of a deep bunker. Maybe another will go ten yards short of the green on an upslope in the fairway. Maybe the third will go into the rough, with a downhill lie. Play each ball to the hole. Putt them all out. Vary the placement of the practice balls on the next hole, but drop your balls from five to twenty yards away from the green. That's the range of the short shots most golfers play during an actual round.

This is the closest you can come to practicing in the physical environment in which your short game will ultimately be tested. You don't hit the same shot twice in a row on the golf course. You have to adjust to a new stance and a new lie on every short shot you hit. Practicing like this is the best way to simulate these factors. The skills you develop with this sort of practice will most readily transfer to competition.

The skills you practice will also transfer better if you can simulate the mental circumstances of competition. The best way to do this is to turn practice into a competition. You can do this when you're alone, but it's even better with a partner.

The late Paul Runyan, who had one of the greatest short games in golf history, showed me a practice game he did religiously. He'd take a single golf ball and drop it in ten different spots around a practice green. He had to hole the ball from the ten situations in twenty shots or fewer. That meant that if he failed to get one up and down, he had to pitch one in to avoid going over twenty. Paul rarely failed at this drill when I watched him. If he did, he started over.

The idea of starting over comes up in a lot of practice-green games. So goes the idea of pitching and then putting, rather than practicing pitches and putts in isolation from one another. You need to put pressure on yourself to simulate the pressure of competition. You need to get accustomed to the idea that a good pitch means nothing unless it leads to a one-putt and that unsatisfactory pitches can be salvaged by a good putt.

Try using one ball for these drills. Again, this simulates the actual game of golf.

Padraig Harrington likes to find another good player and have a competitive game with a little money riding on it. He and his opponent drop a ball in a bunker or in a pitching situation. Their goal is to get their shot into the hole. Pitching the ball into the hole or exploding it out of the bunker and into the hole is worth two points. If no one holes his shot, the player closest to the hole gets a point. If a player holes a pitch or explosion on top of his opponent's, it's worth four points. The first player to five points wins the bet, and another game starts.

I like this kind of practice particularly because it prods a good player like Padraig to go unconscious. He knows that's the best way to pitch the ball in the hole or get it very close. If he were simply out by a practice green, practicing pitch shots, he might be tempted to start thinking about his technique. Padraig is so conscious of this that if he's practicing by himself at a tournament site, he'll make a bet with his caddie, Ronan Flood. Ronan puts up $10 against Padraig picking up the dinner check, and Padraig has to get four out of five balls within tap-in range to win the money. Ronan doesn't mind paying if he has to, because he knows it's making Padraig better, which will pay off for him in the end.

These games can be easily adapted to putting as well. I like to see kids playing putting games against each other. As far as I am concerned, they can do it for hours on end if they want to. It's good for them. But when it comes to routine putting practice of the kind adults generally do, I think the law of diminishing returns quickly takes effect. When a professional player who practices four hours a day asks me how much of his daily practice time he should devote to putting, he's sometimes surprised when I tell him that fifteen to twenty minutes should suffice. I think that when players spend more time that that, a couple of bad things can happen. They can see a lot of putts miss the hole if they putt from long range. Or they can start thinking about their technique when they putt from short range.

I tell players that when they practice, they ought to spend a lot of time putting from inside six feet, so they feel very solid with putts of that length. These putts are critical in almost any round of golf. For the most part, I like to see players putt in places where the ball will break, even on short putts. Use Brad Faxon's drill, rolling the ball into the hole at three different speeds on three different lines.

There are many other drills. Graeme McDowell uses an around-the-world drill, making four consecutive putts from compass points on a circle around the hole. When he makes four in a row, he adds a foot or two to the radius of the circle. Dottie Pepper used a drill where she placed three tees in the ground, one three feet from the hole, one five feet, and one seven feet. She putted from three feet until she'd made three in a row, then putted from five feet until she'd made three more in a row, and then moved back to seven feet and made three in a row. If she missed at any time during this skein of nine putts, she started over from three feet. When an amateur uses this drill, he makes a lot of three-foot putts. He completes it feeling very confident about making putts anywhere inside seven feet. That confidence bolsters every facet of his game.

Though I usually prefer to see players practice breaking putts, I love putting practice that involves straight putts and a chalk line. You can lay down a chalk line with an inexpensive construction tool—essentially a spool of string in a canister of chalk dust. It puts a straight but temporary line on the ground. Use it on a flat section of the practice green and make a line six or eight feet long, beginning at the lip of a cup. Place a ball on the line and putt it. Don't, however, think about forcing your putter blade to move up and back along the line. Just let it. Several good things will happen—what I call the magic of the chalk line.

First, your aim and stroke will be good, even though you won't be thinking about them. This feeling will register in your subconscious brain and will help you later, out on the golf course. Second, you'll sink a lot of putts, probably a lot more six-foot putts than you're accustomed to making. In fact, it's hard to miss them when you use the chalk line. That will help build your confidence. Third, you'll get practice in seeing the line of a putt. It will make you a more visual putter. After they've done this drill, many players tell me they start seeing a chalk line wherever they putt. The chalk line is like training wheels for your visualization skills.

But, again, I'm suggesting five minutes with the chalk line, not hours. Five minutes is enough to get the benefits.

There's a variation on the chalk line idea that has the player stretch a string until it's taut, eight inches above the green, tied to two sticks or pencils. The player putts under the string. I think the chalk line is better because I've never had anyone tell me that after doing the string drill, he goes out on the course and visualizes a string eight inches above the ground.

I would suggest to average players that they then practice for a little while hitting putts from fifteen to forty feet. But don't use a hole as a target. Putt to a coin or a tee in the ground. Putt to the fringe on the edge of the practice green. If you putt to a hole from this distance, you're going to see balls miss, and you don't need to practice missing putts. You're just trying to hone your subconscious brain's sense of how hard you need to strike a putt to make it go a certain distance.

Amateurs generally don't have to spend much time practicing from six feet to fifteen feet. Pros are different. They have to make their share of putts from that range, so they need to practice it. But whether amateur or pro, you need to see yourself making a lot of putts whenever your target is a hole.

THIRTEEN

EXERCISING YOUR MIND

What do I think about when I'm concentrating? I don't know.
I can't think when I'm concentrating.

—Yogi Berra

The first time I ever talked to the late Seve Ballesteros, he had a slightly facetious but intriguing concern. Seve told me about an unusual audiotape that a friend of his had made. It was a full, detailed description of Seve winning the Masters. It was unusual because the friend had made the tape before Seve won his first Masters, in 1980.

The fact that a European could win the Masters no longer strikes anyone as startling. But when Seve did it, no European had ever put on the green jacket. That was a formidable mental barrier. Seve intuitively realized that the tape his friend had made was a way for him to get over that hurdle. He told me that by the time his plane landed in America for that 1980 Masters, he'd listened to the tape thousands of times. When he got off the plane, he already knew he was going to win the Masters.

So what was the problem? I asked.

Seve grinned. He told me that when he'd walked up the 18th fairway that Sunday, he'd felt no excitement. He'd already known he was going to win. All of his excitement had come and gone as he listened to the tape.

I laughed. "Well, I'll teach you how to party after you win," I said.

Seve, in his intuitive, naturally gifted way, had figured out something I was teaching my graduate students in sports psychology at the University of Virginia. Practicing with the mind can be just as important as physical practice.

Your conscious mind programs your subconscious mind. The thoughts and ideas that you have about golf, the conversations you have about golf, and the things people say to you about your golf are all retained somewhere in the brain, often below the level of conscious thought. This offers you a tremendous opportunity. You can be the producer, director, and screenwriter of your own autobiographical movie.

I don't mean that you can simply daydream your way to fortune and fame. Golf doesn't work that way. Golfing skill is composed in equal measure of competence and confidence. A player needs both. In the last chapter, I presented my thoughts about physical practice and I suggested, among other things, that you practice pitching the ball from bad lies. But when you can hit good practice pitches off the tightest lies you can find, you're not necessarily ready for competition. You must also have developed confidence, the solid belief that you can transfer this skill to the golf course during a tournament. If you don't have the confidence, your physical skill in the practice area will remain only there—in the practice area.

Obviously, it helps your confidence if you can see yourself hitting good shot after good shot in the practice area. But you need more. You need to believe in yourself in the clutch, at whatever level of competition you aspire to win. You can help yourself achieve this kind of confidence off the golf course. That's why I suggest you can write and produce your own autobiography. Just as Seve Ballesteros did with his friend's tape, you can use your conscious mind to program your subconscious mind to perform reliably in stressful situations. And you can practice doing this.

One form of mental practice is meditation. Sometimes a player will tell me that no matter how hard he tries, he can't seem to clear his mind before a shot or during visualization. Thoughts are always zipping around in his conscious brain. **My response is that if you want a quiet mind you have to practice having a quiet mind.**

Sit down in a quiet, darkened room. Turn your phone off and make sure you won't be distracted. Make a conscious effort to focus all your attention on something. It can be your breathing, your heart rate, a ceiling tile, or your big toe. If it's your breathing, hear the air moving in and out of your lungs. Feel the way your rib cage expands and contracts. Consider the way the oxygen replenishes your body. Consider how your body and brain don't need you to tell them to breathe. You just do it. Feel each breath. Keep doing it. Feel your mind grow calmer, quieter. Make this a part of your daily routine and you will be training your mind to achieve the clear and uncluttered state you want when you play golf.

I've already described another aspect of mental practice, the visualization techniques you can use off the golf course. As you now know, it's important to make these imagined experiences as vivid as possible. If you're the sort who worries about his golf when he's off the course, this is a way to use that worry productively. Use it as a motivation to spend some time concentrating on vivid visualization.

Be persistent with it. Sometimes a client will call me a week or so after I have suggested he try visualization. He's about to give up. "I've tried to see myself winning, doing my routine, hitting shots, making putts," he'll say. "I get so nervous just thinking about it that I totally lose control of my visualization. I can't see it."

I respond, "Well, if you can't even lie in bed and imagine it, how do you think you're going to control your mind and emotions enough actually to do it? **If someone asked you to change your golf swing and you tried it for four days and didn't see any progress, would you abandon the effort and decide it couldn't work? You wouldn't! You'd keep at it because you know that a change like that takes time. It's the same thing with visualization. Keep practicing until you can control the images that enter your mind."**

I have made audio recordings for players to help them visualize. They can transfer them to their iPods and listen at night before they fall asleep. Here's a transcript of one that many winning golfers have listened to. You could record it and play it for yourself, using the words to help create pictures in your mind.

> *Pretend you're lying outside on a nice, warm day and the sun has just come out from behind a cloud. Feel the sun and its heat as it touches your forehead. Your forehead gets very relaxed. The sun hits your eyelids and you feel your eyelids get very warm and very heavy. The sun goes down onto your shoulders and they get very relaxed, heavy, and warm. Feel*

that sun slowly go down your entire body and let your entire body feel very at ease, very calm, and very relaxed. Enjoy how good that feels.

Now I want you to visualize yourself at a tournament. It's Sunday. You're playing the back nine. See yourself paired in a group with two of the best players in the world, feeling proud of how good you are, feeling very confident in yourself, very happy and sure of yourself, because this is where you want to be. This is where you know you belong, knowing that you were born to play golf and destined to be a great player. Just enjoy how good it feels to realize that all the years of practice and development have made you one of the best players in the world. Now here you are in the last group, with the whole world enjoying watching you play.

You're very happy. You're filled with joy. You're just enjoying the good feeling of playing great golf.

See yourself very clearly, hitting beautiful shots with a very quiet mind. Over the ball, all you ever do is see it and hit it. On the putting green, you just see it and roll it. Wedge shots over a bunker to a tight pin—there is no thinking. Your mind is so quiet. You just see the shot and do it, totally trusting that the ball will go to the hole. If you miss a green occasionally, it doesn't bother you in the least because you know you have a great short game. You just walk up to the ball, thinking about pitching it in the hole. You just enjoy how good it feels to be such a solid player.

You know that you're strong mentally and emotionally. You're like a rock. Nothing bothers you or upsets you. You may miss a shot or two. Everyone does. Those mistakes mean noth-

ing to you. You attach no emotion to them. You play the next shot as if it's the beginning of a new round. You never waver from your commitment to just see it and hit it, all day.

You play happy. You enjoy allowing yourself to be yourself and play within your personality. In between shots you're talking to your caddie and to your playing partners, and you're comfortable, because this is where you want to be. All day on that back nine you just keep looking for something good to happen until you find a good break that you knew was coming your way, because you know you're destined to win a number of tournaments this year. You look for a good bounce, you look for a putt to lip in. You can't help but think of how great your swing feels and how much joy you have playing golf, because this is your game. This is what you're most gifted at. This is the game that you love and enjoy.

As you walk down the fairway you have a joyful mind and a playful mood. You really feel that you're playing a game that you love. But you regularly remind yourself and your caddie that your only goal is to think the same way on every shot—you're going to see it and hit it and see it and roll it. Nothing is going to become more important than that.

On your putts, all you care about is that you see it and roll it. You have total trust in your abilities and in your talents. You have undying patience, and the reason you have so much patience is because you have a quiet mind and you went to the first tee today knowing how you were going to think every time you stood over a golf shot. That makes you feel so good, because you know that if you just think the same way all day and trust yourself, winning will happen. You understand that this is a key to winning—playing one shot at a time, accepting it wherever it goes, finding it, and doing it again.

Your mind is very quiet over the ball because you love your talent and you love your game. You're enjoying trusting your instincts. You watch other players overthinking their club selection, worrying about being long and short, and you're having so much fun just trusting what you're doing. You're just loving your game and enjoying how good that feels, just seeing it and doing it. On the putting greens you're constantly trusting your instinct. You're seeing it and rolling it. You love how well your instinct works. You enjoy how easy it is to read the greens when you're just going with your first instinct. You're trusting your first instinct with a quiet mind because you love how good your eyes are and how well you can read greens when you trust yourself and are looking to make it. You're enjoying the fact that you never worry about running it by or leaving it short. You just enjoy seeing it and rolling it. It's the most wonderful, playful feeling in the world.

Play is very slow today and the other players in your group are starting to complain and getting uptight about it. But you're just happy. Nothing is taking you out of this mood. You know that nothing is going to bother you or upset you. You're having fun being here because this is where you belong. You know it gives you an edge when you see them get bothered and upset. They make a mistake and let it fluster them. Nothing bothers you.

Maybe it's windy out. You decide that you love the wind, because you're a great golfer. Your mind's going to be in con-

trol. You're not going to let the wind control your mind. You're going to let your mind control the wind. The more elements there are that bother other players, the better you feel. But if it's a perfect day, you love playing in perfect conditions, because you know with your mind you're going to let yourself go low and make lots of birdies. You're going to stay out of your way and have a calm, quiet mind. You're going to spend the entire day just seeing it and rolling it.

You love the challenge of the game. The challenge is against yourself and the golf course. It's just you and your ball and the golf course. You really don't care about anything else. The better you play, the calmer you get. The more birdies you make, the quieter your mind gets, the more at ease you are, the more you enjoy the game. You love how good it feels to be seeing it and doing it, because you know when everything's going your way, you just put it on autopilot and run with it. You're not going to analyze it. You're not going to make sure you keep it going. Or make sure you don't lose it. You're just going to see it and do it and love how good it feels. As you've learned, this is what playing golf is all about. This is what playing with confidence is all about. You can now see so clearly in your mind that golf is a game and it has to be played.

You have a putt from twelve feet on the last green. Everyone's trying to tell you what it's for, that it will give you your first win. You collect yourself and remind yourself that your only objective is the same as it was on the first green on Thursday, and that is to see it and roll it with a quiet mind. Because you know that if you can do that, you are a winner and you're going to win your share of tournaments. It feels so good when you know what you're going to do, when you just see it and roll it and see the ball go in the hole.

You see the smile, the feeling of satisfaction as you get the ball out of the hole, hug your caddie, accept congratulations. You can see yourself accepting the check and holding the trophy up. You can see yourself giving a talk. You can see yourself calling home and telling your family and friends. You enjoy how good it feels. But what you're most proud of is how relaxed you were and how much fun you had and how much you trusted yourself. You know there are going to be many more days like this, because for the rest of your career you're going to let the game be this simple and have this much fun playing. Because now you know that when you're having fun and just seeing it and doing it, winning happens. That's the real secret to the game of golf. Anything your mind can conceive you will allow yourself to do. As long as you can see the shot, you will allow yourself to hit it. As long as you can see the putt, you can make it. You love how good that feels.

Now very slowly open your eyes and take a couple of deep breaths to get yourself back in the present.

As with any other sort of practice, the rewards for mental practice tend to reflect the effort that you put into them. If you're lackadaisical about it, you won't see much change. But if you work hard at mental practice, I think you'll be pleasantly surprised at the way it will improve your game. Never underestimate the power of your mind.

FOURTEEN

THE PAYOFF

The golfer who lacks confidence in his short game puts a tremendous burden on himself when it comes to playing full shots to the green.

—Paul Runyan

On the day before the 2011 British Open, I saw Darren Clarke on the putting green at Royal St. George's and said hello.

"Man, we really need to talk," he said.

Darren, I would learn, was feeling bad about his short game, specifically his putting. His frustration with it was spilling over into his attitude toward his game in general.

I had known Darren for many years and we'd worked together before. I like and admire him, so I was happy to do what I could to listen and help. We walked off the putting green to an enclosure reserved for Royal St. George's members, next to the clubhouse. It was chilly and cold and we sat down in a corner that was sheltered from the wind.

The members were more than happy to share their enclosure with Darren. He's a beloved figure throughout the British Isles, where they remember the stoic gallantry with which he bore the pain of losing his wife, Heather, to cancer, and the stellar golf he has given to the European side in many Ryder Cup matches.

The chairman of the Royal St. George's green committee came up to Darren and introduced himself. Darren complimented him on the superb condition of the course, which set the man smiling, and he volunteered to fetch Darren a cup of coffee. Other members approached, almost shyly, and said that while they didn't want to interrupt, they would greatly appreciate it if Darren would sign this hat, or that flag, or this program. Darren obliged them all with a smile, and in between scrawling his signature, he told me how he was feeling.

"I'm nice to everyone else," he said, after signing another autograph. "But I'm miserable to myself and with myself. Right now, I feel like I hate the game."

That was not what I like to hear a player saying on the eve of a major championship. I hadn't seen Darren during the previous couple of years as often as I once did, because he was rarely in the United States. His position in the golf rankings had fallen below the level that got him automatic entry into the world golf championship events and the major tournaments, most of which are played in America. He was forty-two; once he'd been the bright young hope of Irish golf, but by the summer of 2011, there were golf writers who thought his time had passed. Younger Irish golfers—Padraig Harrington, Graeme McDowell, Rory McIlroy—had in fact seemed to surpass him. I'd spent time with each of them, and they'd all won major championships. Darren was genuinely happy for each of them, and he'd celebrated with each of them. But their major titles had made him want one of his own all the more.

I had kept up with him enough to know that he'd seen some recent positive changes in his life. He'd moved his two boys, Tyrone and Conor, from London back to Northern Ireland, and they were playing a lot of golf together at his home course, Royal Portrush. He'd recently become engaged. And he'd won a European Tour event, the Iberdrola Open, in the middle of May. It had been his first win since 2008, and so I'd expected, if anything, that Darren would be happy and optimistic at Royal St. George's. I asked him what had happened.

"Instead of milking my win, I've screwed everything up," he said. "I'm trying to make everything perfect. I'm trying to live up to the win. I am working so hard on my golf swing and trying to make it perfect. I'm working even harder trying to make my putting stroke perfect. I've tried turning my hands over on an arc. I've tried leaning the handle forward. I've tried so many things different teachers have told me."

This was a story I was familiar with. You might think that when a player wins a tournament, especially a major championship, he would react by thinking, *Finally, I've got my swing and my putting stroke so good that I can stop worrying about them, go unconscious, and keep winning*. Instead, what many players think is, *Wow! Winning means I'm exempt from having to qualify for two years* [or five years, if it's a major]. *I'll use that time to reconstruct my swing and my stroke and make them perfect*. But that effort can wreak havoc with a player's game and confidence. It had with Darren.

"The more I lean the shaft, the more I push-block all my putts," he said. "If I worry about push-blocking them, I pull them. Nothing

I try works, and the harder I practice, the worse I feel and play. I hit it worse and I putt it worse. I even try different approaches to putting during the middle of a round. I just keep doing it and it's driving me crazy."

Darren thought that if he and I could repair his attitude toward putting, it would take the pressure off his ball-striking and his short game. He would no longer feel that he had to aim at the pin with every approach shot and hit every pitch to a foot if he wanted to make birdies. That's the way getting careful with putting can infect other areas of the game. Darren was normally a great pitcher of the golf ball. His full swing produced low, powerful shots that were ideally suited to windy links golf. But his worries about his putting undermined those other skills.

"I'm really okay on my three- to four-foot putts," he went on. "But I don't make any ten- to fifteen-foot putts." Those are the putts top professionals count on to make birdies. "And my speed control is terrible on longer ones. I feel like I never find the middle of my putter face and I can't get the ball started on line or find the right speed on the long ones."

He very much wanted to play his best at this Open and to validate his May triumph in Spain. Yet his desire seemed only to exacerbate his frustration. Instead of optimistic, he felt tired and disappointed. Darren is always filled with energy, but sometimes it's positive energy that propels him to great things, and sometimes it's a kind of negative energy that can deflate him.

I looked at him and said, "Darren, all I know is you were a helluva putter as a teenager. I know you could putt brilliantly when you were sixteen, seventeen years old."

"Yeah, I could," he said.

"That means you already know how to putt," I said. "You have to stop pretending you don't know how to putt. If you stopped pretending you don't know how to putt, you'd stop trying to do it 'correctly,' and you'd just do it your way."

"I don't even know what my way is anymore. I've tried so many things," Darren said.

"You've got to stop trying so hard to do it 'correctly' and trying so hard to make it that you're forcing it and gunning your putts way past the hole," I said. "Then on the next one you give up on it and leave it a mile short because you're worried about running it way past. You've got to get a little bit more of a Tom Watson attitude, where he just sees it and hits it and accepts it wherever it goes. Stop trying to be so darn perfect and controlling of everything."

I suggested to Darren that he needed to get all the technical and mechanical ideas out of his mind as he putted and just unconsciously react to his target.

"Oh, Doc, I'd love to go unconscious. I love the idea of going unconscious, but at the same time it scares the heck out of me. I've been so conscious for so long."

"If you believed you knew how to putt, you would go unconscious and let it go," I said. "If you were convinced you didn't know how to putt and have never known how to putt, then you would need to turn on your conscious brain and try to control it.

"We need to go back to some basics," I went on. "We need to review some things we haven't talked about in a long time."

I stood up and asked Darren to take a golf ball and throw it to me. I held up my hand. He hit my hand. I said, "Good. Do it some more." He tossed a few more to me as I moved forward and back, giving him different distances to toss it. All of his tosses, of course, came right to my hand, softly enough that I caught them easily.

"You just looked at my hand and you threw it," I said. "Did you ever think of aiming the palm of your hand when you threw the ball to me?"

"No," Darren said.

"Did you ever look at your hand to see if it was aimed correctly?"

"No."

"Did you ever tell yourself how hard to throw it, or how far to take your arm back, or how to stand or where your weight was?"

"No."

"Yet you got the ball right to my hand every time, with just the right speed. With throwing a ball you totally trust yourself."

I asked him to think back on what had happened when we'd first come into the members' enclosure and began to talk. "Every time you signed an autograph for someone, you didn't even look at what you were signing. You were looking at me and talking to me. And yet every time, your name came out and the people were happy. While we were sitting there talking, you drank that coffee one of the members got for you. It was amazing. You were looking at me, you were talking about golf, and yet you didn't spill anything on your pants. How the hell did you know where your mouth was?"

Darren smiled.

"It's like watching a really good pianist at a concert. The person is just hearing the music in her head and her hands are going a hundred miles an hour, and she's just responding to what she's hearing in her mind. Yet she never hits a wrong key unless she starts thinking consciously about hitting the right key or starts worrying about hitting the wrong key."

I reminded him of the last time I'd visited his home. We'd played soccer with his boys, who were then around the ages of six and four. When we'd kicked the ball to the boys, we never instructed ourselves on what to do with our feet or how far ahead of them to kick the ball. We'd just seen them moving and done it.

"Now you're playing a lot of golf with your kids. You're going to be amazed at how easy everything I am asking you to do will be for them to do. Your kids will never say we won't have fun playing golf today if we don't break 90. You've got to have that attitude. But as we grow up and rise in the golf world, somehow we get obsessed with results. We get educated into trusting our conscious mind more than our subconscious mind, even when we're doing things we're very skilled at," I said.

I told him about a program I had done for the National Stuttering Association and how many stutterers speak perfectly well when they're alone but start stuttering when they feel social pressure and worry about making a verbal mistake.

I told Darren that Michael Jordan, in a recent book, dismissed the notion of fear, at least as it pertains to athletics. Fear is a mirage, an illusion, Jordan said. Nothing bad really happens. But a lot of people, when they fear playing badly, turn on their conscious minds. **Instead, they need to remember that golf is a game, and it must be played. There's nothing to fear from a game.**

"In order to play the game, you've got to be athletic," I told Darren. **"An athletic mind is an unconscious mind. The willingness to go unconscious and to trust yourself as a skilled golfer and athlete**

will be how you separate yourself from others. That's all I mean by letting go of conscious control and letting your talent loose. You've got plenty of talent, but in order to turn it loose you've got to let go of conscious control. **You've got to get out there in the target and just unconsciously react or respond. I can't completely explain why, but when you're gifted at something, and you just look at a target and let go, your body responds by sending the ball there. And this is what you're talented at."**

I reminded Darren that we had talked a lot during his career about being his own best friend and trying less. "You've been trying too hard, Darren, and that's not trying your best."

I introduced Darren to the name Vince Lombardi, the great American football coach, and his maxim that fatigue makes cowards of us all. "You have to be rested or you won't be able to handle all the things this tournament is going to throw at you. You don't need to spend seven hours a day here practicing. You already know how to play golf. You need to chill. You don't need to spend every daylight hour here trying to find your game. It's already inside you."

At that point, Darren pulled out his phone and said, "Repeat that, please. I want to make a note for myself. I like that, because, man, I have been so tired. Even when I'm practicing, I'm exhausted."

Then Darren asked me, "Well, how does Padraig Harrington do this? I love him to death, but I know he's more analytical than I am."

I said, "Well, Darren, you're right. But when it's time to play golf, he turns it loose and gets less analytical. When it's time to play golf, you get more analytical. Padraig asks a lot of questions, because he wants to understand things. But once he understands them, he can go unconscious really well."

I asked Darren to come over to the putting green. I told him to casually look at the target and hit his putts. If the target was two inches right of the cup, I wanted him to casually look out there to the right and not to try to stare at a spot exactly two inches away. Then I wanted him to let whatever happened happen.

Darren did that for a while, and he said, "That feels pretty good. It feels like I'm hitting the ball right in the middle of my putter face."

I told Darren then about some of the things I've learned from Ben Crenshaw about putting. Crenshaw feels like when he gets to Augusta he can putt great, because the greens are so slick that he can make every putt on any of six or seven lines, depending on the speed he hits it. Ben feels that he can give up control at Augusta and just putt on a line that feels good to him. He makes a lot of putts that way.

"Darren, let's hit some now and I don't want you even to try to do a routine."

His ears perked up. He knew that I'd always stressed the importance of a routine.

"If all you did was casually look out there and then unconsciously let whatever happened happen, everyone watching you would say you had a great routine on every putt. But I don't want you *try* to do a routine. Just casually look at a target, unconsciously let it go, and let what happens happen. Just see it and roll it and you'll be amazed at how your speed and line will get better."

Darren rolled in a few that way and remarked again how it felt like he was finally making contact with the ball in the middle of his putter blade. I didn't want him to care about where the blade met the ball. So I asked him to putt a few using the toe of the putter. He made four or five in a row. Then I asked him to use the heel of the putter and he rolled some in that way, too. Then I had him twist the putter 90 degrees in his hand and make them with the point of the putter. He did that.

"Putters today are so well made the whole face is pretty damn solid. It really doesn't matter where you hit it," I said. "You've got to understand that solid contact will happen if you stop trying to hit it in the middle of the putter face. And the more you don't care about hitting it in the middle of the face, the easier it is to hit it in the middle of the face."

Darren stroked a few more putts that way, and he told me he really loved the way he felt when he did it. But he was still being analytical about his stroke. "I feel some wristiness and some release, but I'm not trying to release it," he said.

As I've told you, you can find half a dozen putting experts who will define "release" in half a dozen different ways. I didn't even ask Darren what he thought it meant. By "wristiness," he meant that he thought he could feel his wrists hinge during the stroke. A lot of putting instructors advocate moving the club without wrist action.

"You feel what you feel," I said. "Just let whatever happens happen," I said.

I would never try to tell him what he should feel, because then he'd start worrying about whether he was feeling what I said he should feel. That would be the opposite of putting unconsciously. I could tell Darren found the concept of letting whatever happened in his stroke happen to be both interesting and mind-boggling. I wanted him just to stop worrying about the mechanics of the putting stroke, but we weren't quite there yet.

I asked him to toss some balls to me again from varying distances, just as he had in the members' enclosure. "Darren, all I can tell you is that when you stand four or five feet away, I don't see much wrist action. But at a certain distance, your wrists start to hinge. It's instinctive for an athlete. Release will happen when it's supposed to happen. Don't pay any attention to it, or try to do it, or care about it. Let whatever happens happen."

I could see he was starting to understand and agree.

I used the same analogy to bunker play with Darren that I had used with David Frost. Darren is an excellent bunker player. When I asked him, he confirmed that he was unconscious of things like how much he opened up his clubface in a bunker or how he adjusted his stance. He just did those things and the ball went where he was looking.

He hit practice putts from a variety of distances. His speed was great on all of them, except on the occasions when he started being conscious of the speed. Then he tended to leave them short or run them well past. The more we did it, the more I saw an amazed look on his face. He was putting well without thinking about things he had gotten accustomed to thinking about. "I don't even know what my stance is, or where my weight is, or what my posture is," he said.

"Good. I don't want you to. You're doing great. Just look where you want it to go and let it happen. That's how you drive your car. That's how you played rugby when you were good at it. That's how you do every physical activity except the one you love the most and you're best at. When you turn on your conscious brain on the golf course, you get in the way of your talent. You deprive yourself of your talent," I said.

"I want you to putt as if you've left your conscious brain in the locker room and taped over all the air vents in the locker. I want you to putt with your eyes and your instinct. That's what I mean by putting unconsciously. Look where you want it to go, then hit it instinctively, and we're going to call it a beautiful putting stroke."

Darren indeed putted beautifully on Thursday, shooting a 68, three strokes off the pace. The next day, on the practice green, he told me that he had gone back to his rented house and watched himself putt on the evening television recap of the day's play. He said he was amazed by the disparity between the way his stroke looked on TV and the way it had felt on the course. On tape, he saw quiet hands—no wristiness, no flipping. He'd loved the way his stroke looked. That wasn't how it had felt on the course.

"What I'm feeling and what I'm doing aren't necessarily the same," he said. "But yesterday, I hit every putt in the middle of the face and started it on line. My speed was immediately great. I haven't done that for so long."

"I don't know why that would surprise you," I said. "That's your gift, your talent. You've got to ride your talent, milk your talent. It will take you to heaven if you let it. But you have to stop trying to control it."

The change in Darren's putting was apparent in his scores. He shot a 68 the second day and tied for the lead with Lucas Glover. But the reason for the change wasn't readily apparent to the galleries, the television audience, or the press. One reporter called me on Friday and asked whether I agreed that the improvement in Darren's putting was due to a tip he'd gotten from a putting instructor about not taking practice strokes while he was over the ball. It wasn't, but I couldn't get the journalist to understand or accept the fact that Darren hadn't been guided to the "perfect" putting routine. Just the opposite. He'd stopped the futile quest for perfection, and when he'd done that, his putting improved. That's how you get from good to great.

I saw Darren again on Saturday before he teed off. At this stage in an event, I can't really teach a player too much. I try to give players a few thoughts that they can carry around the golf course with them. Golf gives its players a lot of time to think between shots. I want them to think about something that will help them. I want to help them relax and think confidently.

"You're unstoppable if you're unflappable," I told Darren. "Surrender to your talent. Ride your talent. It's there. It's inside you. Just get out of your way and let it happen. There's a big difference between letting it happen and trying to make it happen. You're only trying to make it happen if you're worried that winning isn't going to happen. Letting it happen is closely related to being happy and patient. You know how happy and patient you would be if you knew that you were destined to play great? Be that way. It's hard to do because letting it happen can make you feel like you're not trying enough and you're very used to trying hard. If you're just enjoying the challenge and relishing the challenge, and letting it happen, believe me that you'll be doing all you can do to get what you want. You may think you're not trying, but everyone else is going to be seeing you as cool, calm, and collected."

As we walked toward the first tee, the applause from the gallery, packed into bleachers and lining the rope corridor that linked green and tee, overwhelmed us both for a moment. I said, "Darren, you know that all of these guys that you're playing with are guys who love the game as much as you do. It's like going to a party with your best friends. When you walk in the door, you've got a big grin on your face because you're excited about whom you're going to see. That's how I want you to feel."

On Saturday, Darren shot 69 and took the lead by a stroke over Dustin Johnson.

On Sunday, I spent most of my time on the putting green, talking to players before they went to the first tee. Darren would be one of the last players to finish warming up on the range and come over to hit some practice putts before his round. I wondered what his demeanor would be. When I caught sight of him, I was thrilled because he had a broad grin on his face. He was unhurried, like a man who owned Royal St. George's rather than a man with a looming tee time for the most important round of his career. He signed autographs for a hoard of kids, making eye contact with each kid and letting them help him be in a great mood.

The sight reminded me of how Padraig Harrington had been just before winning his second British Open at Royal Birkdale in 2008. I loved seeing Darren in that state of mind, and I really felt good about his chances.

I gave him a big smile and a high five. "Darren, it's party time."

He told me he felt great, but then he mentioned that on Saturday, he'd been very nervous on the first six holes because the reception by the gallery on the first tee had been so long, loud, and warm that it had touched him deeply. He felt he'd gotten conscious and careful on the first birdie putts he'd had. He'd wound up leaving them short. He'd gotten untracked on the 7th hole and stayed unconscious through the end of the third round. I didn't want him to get started picking his play apart. I told him how much I loved the way he'd managed his emotions, how he'd gotten looser and freer as the round had progressed.

"Your last five putts were fabulous," I said. On the last hole of the third round, he had made a 20-foot birdie putt uphill to a back pin. I had seen several other players leave that putt short. Darren had run his putt five feet past, but he'd merely stepped up to the next putt and casually rolled it in. It reminded me of Nancy Lopez telling me that in her prime she loved running putts way by the hole, because her opponents would get flustered when she banged the return putt home.

"That's what I was thinking of when you were telling me about how you felt putting," I said. I reflected with him about Brad Faxon, a great putter, and two of Brad's ideas on the greens. **One was caring less as the round went on; the second was seeing great putts that didn't go in as great putts.** "If you get your mind in the right place, then roll the ball, it's a great putt because you made it in your mind, then went unconscious," I said. "If you keep doing that, your putting will always range from good to great. Don't be dependent on the ball going in the hole to make you feel great about your putting. A lot of guys do that on Sunday and they turn good putts into bad putts and use that to justify getting conscious and careful. So let's really stay out of your way. But if you do get in your way on a couple of shots, just accept it. Don't beat yourself up and don't get mad. Just keep smiling and milk the crowd all you can and just enjoy the moment. And if you catch yourself getting careful and getting conscious, just walk away and break up laughing and tell yourself, 'You silly son of a buck. Come on now. I know how to do this. Now just see it and do it.' Let's win the battle with yourself and just see it and do it."

Darren said, "You know, Doc, I'm going to forget about scoreboards and the other players. I'm going to just love being in my own little world, chatting with my caddie and Dustin and his caddie. I'm just going to have a ball. I'm going to enjoy the day."

I liked hearing that.

For the next few minutes, Darren shared with me a raft of thoughts, marshaling the positive out of all the things he was thinking, out of all the messages he'd received. My job was just to listen.

He talked for a few moments about his wife, Heather, who passed away in 2006. "You know, Doc, I'm a lot more mature since my wife died. It was a real tragedy and a tough time in my life, but I've been through some tough times, and I could sure use a break."

I reminded Darren that he needed to feel destined and to believe that good things would come if he stayed out of his way and waited for them. Tom Watson had once said, "If you want to win, you have to be really good at waiting, and in order to wait, you have to accept." Then Darren turned these sad reflections into something positive. He recalled the 2006 Ryder Cup, at the K Club outside Dublin, shortly after Heather's death. Nothing in his life, he said, had made him as nervous as playing in that Ryder Cup. He was confident that nothing would happen in the final round to equal that pressure.

Darren pulled his phone out of his pocket. "I want to show you something, Doc," he said. It was a text message from Tiger Woods, who'd missed the British Open because of his injured leg. Tiger and Darren had a long competitive history together and a strong friendship. I was impressed that Tiger would reach out to him. It meant a lot to Darren to have Tiger's support.

Darren said he wasn't certain he should let me read the text. "It sounds a lot like what we've been talking about," Darren said, paraphrasing for me. "Tiger says, 'It's a process. Go out there and believe in yourself. Make some early birdies, then stay in the present and play one shot at a time. You know how to do this. Go out there and get it done. Enjoy your day. I'll be rooting for you.'"

Darren had good wishes, too, from his fellow Irishmen Graeme McDowell and Rory McIlroy. Rory had sent him a text that mirrored one that Darren had sent Rory on the night before the final round of the 2011 U.S. Open. Like Tiger's, it said, "Go out there and get it done."

"You know, Darren," I said, "you've always believed in your friends. They obviously believe in you. Now it's time for you to believe in Darren. Just remember how good your touch is when you're unconscious, and all the great putts and pitches and bunker shots you've hit this week. Let's turn the big dog loose, let's go unconscious, and let's have a ball. Let's love the gallery and let's love your playing partner [Dustin Johnson] and let's have a great time out there. Let yourself be yourself. Stop judging yourself, stop judging your round, stop trying to predict how you're going to go, and just play the game. Let winning fall in your lap."

We walked toward the first tee. The applause was thunderous. I loved how he looked at the crowd and acknowledged their applause, how he shook hands with all the people who would be part of his group. Darren was being Darren. He made a good twelve-foot putt for par on the first hole. I was so happy that he'd let himself go unconscious. Then he made a few five-footers, and I knew he was off and running, looking great.

Though Darren didn't want to look at scoreboards, there was nothing to stop me from doing so. I could see that Phil Mickelson had played the first ten holes in six shots under par. Dustin Johnson was only a stroke or two behind. But then Darren made a bomb to eagle the 7th and go to seven under par for the tournament. I was walking along, cheering for Darren to stay out of his own way. As soon as Darren made that eagle, Phil missed a couple of short putts. Dustin hit a ball out of bounds on the 14th.

Winning was indeed falling into Darren's lap.

The party on Sunday night after the tournament was at a house rented by Darren's management company, International Sports Management. I talked to Darren's mother and father and to his fiancée, Alison. They told me they couldn't get over how relaxed Darren had been throughout the tournament. I smiled.

Darren said to me, "I was totally unconscious until the 17th when my caddie told me I had a 5-shot lead. As soon as I found out, I almost purposely got a little conscious and left the putt short and made bogey. On eighteen, I bombed it down the middle but got conscious on my second shot because I knew the tournament was over. I made a bogey. I would love to play those last two holes over and stay unconscious."

But Darren knew better than to beat himself up over that sort of lapse. "I can't tell you how glad I am to have won a major, but I think it's fair to say that I'm even happier that I got out of my way for all four days in a major championship. That's what I'm really proud of.

"I realize now that I'm not too old to win these things and that if I let myself, I can win a lot more of them," Darren said. "It really helped a lot that I didn't put pressure on myself during the weekend. I did a great job of telling myself I just wanted to be in the right state of mind. I didn't constantly tell myself I have to win this because I may never get another chance."

I agreed. I believe Darren can win more major championships. I don't, of course, know whether he will. But I know that if he continues to control his mind and emotions the way he did at the 2011 British Open, he'll be a winner even if he's not always the winner.

I should note here that I don't always get my clients to the place that Darren reached with my help that week at Royal St. George's. I was reminded of that when Padraig Harrington missed the cut at the same tournament. Padraig and I have worked together for many years. Padraig understands what he has to do and he's very good at doing it. But he didn't that week.

After that unsuccessful British Open, Padraig and I talked. Padraig said he thought that the laser eye surgeries he's had over the past few years had in a curious way affected his focus. He hadn't quite gotten used to the changes in his vision. He realized that he didn't quite trust the way his eyes told him the greens would break. He was second-guessing some of his reads just before he started to putt the ball, making minute adjustments. That kind of indecision, at the level of major championship golf, can make the difference between winning and going home early.

What happened to Padraig serves as a reminder that it's not enough to know how to think about your short game. That's the easy part. The hard part is putting into practice what you know.

But if you've read this far attentively, you now understand that the ideas I conveyed to Darren Clarke during the week of the 2011 British Open were the same ideas I've put into this book. They're ideas that can help any golfer, at any level. You may never be able to hit the ball as powerfully as Darren. But you can think the way a great pro does. You can go unconscious on your putts and pitches and bunker shots. In doing so, you can take your game from good to great, however you define greatness.

If you do, you'll be an unstoppable golfer, because, as you now know, you are the only one who can stop you.

The question is, will you stop yourself, or will you let yourself go unconscious? Will you apply your free will to your golf game? Will you think like a champion? I can't guarantee that if you do, you'll be the winner at your next important competition. But I can guarantee that you'll walk off the course at the end of the competition proud and happy with the way you played. You will have stacked the deck in your favor.

You'll be a winner.

ACKNOWLEDGMENTS

I am indebted to many people for help with this book.

My colleague Bob Christina helped enormously with ideas and information about the development of motor skills. Bob teaches in North Carolina, at the Pinehurst Golf Academy in Pinehurst and at Robert Linville's Precision Golf School in Greensboro. Any golfer could benefit from spending time with Bob Christina.

It's been my privilege to work with many of the world's greatest golfers over the years. Several of them were especially helpful for this book. Trevor Immelman, Graeme McDowell, Mark Wilson, Darren Clarke, Peter Uihlein, Pat Bradley, and Keegan Bradley were generous with their time and their memories. Tom Kite, Padraig Harrington, Davis Love III, David Frost, and Brad Faxon have been more than clients over the years; they've been friends. I'd like to thank some of my clients from the amateur ranks for their help, particularly Marty Jacobson and Gary Burkhead. I've learned from every player I've worked with, and what I've taken from them is in the pages of this book. Thanks to them all.

My literary agent, Rafe Sagalyn, and my editor, Dominick Anfuso, have been genuine partners for seventeen years, as they were on this project.

And, finally, none of what I do would be possible without my wife, Darlene.

ABOUT THE AUTHORS

Dr. Bob Rotella is one of the world's preeminent sports psychologists and performance coaches. He specializes in helping golfers overcome their mental challenges. Golfers coached by Bob Rotella have won a total of 74 major championships. He has also helped athletes in tennis, baseball, basketball and other sports as well as singers and business leaders.

Dr. Rotella got his bachelor's degree from Castleton State College in Vermont and his doctorate from the University of Connecticut. He was the Director of Sports Psychology at the University of Virginia for 20 years, a period in which he helped the Cavaliers' football and basketball programs rise from decades of losing seasons to participation in bowl games and NCAA tournaments. He and his wife, Darlene, live in Virginia.

Bob Cullen is a journalist and writer. During the years he has collaborated with Dr. Bob Rotella, his golf handicap has gone from 21 to 5. He lives with his wife, Ann, in Chevy Chase, Maryland.